**Cultural and
Geographical
Exploration**

Rediscovering Ancient Egypt

CHRONICLES FROM *NATIONAL GEOGRAPHIC*

Cultural and Geographical Exploration

Cultural and Geographical Exploration

Rediscovering Ancient Eygypt

CHRONICLES FROM *NATIONAL GEOGRAPHIC*

Arthur M. Schlesinger, jr.
Senior Consulting Editor

Fred L. Israel
General Editor

CHELSEA HOUSE PUBLISHERS

Philadelphia

CHELSEA HOUSE PUBLISHERS

Editor in Chief Stephen Reginald
Managing Editor James D. Gallagher
Production Manager Pamela Loos
Art Director Sara Davis
Director of Photography Judy L. Hasday
Senior Production Editor LeeAnne Gelletly

The Chelsea House World Wide Web site address is
http://www.chelseahouse.com

First Printing

1 3 5 7 9 8 6 4 2

Library of Congress Cataloging-in-Publication Data

  Rediscovering ancient Egypt.
      p. cm. – (Cultural and geographic exploration: chronicles
    from National Geographic)
    Includes index.
    ISBN 0-7910-5445-4 (hc)
    1. Egypt—Antiquities Juvenile literature.   2. Egypt—
    Civilization—To 332 B.C. Juvenile literature.
    I. National Geographic Society (U.S.)
    II. Series: Cultural and geographical exploration.
    DT60.R395   1999
    932—dc21   99-24269
                                            CIP

CONTENTS

"THE GREATEST EDUCATIONAL JOURNAL"

When the first *National Geographic* magazine appeared in October 1888, the United States totaled 38 states. Grover Cleveland was President. The nation's population hovered around 60 million. Great Britain's Queen Victoria also ruled as the Empress of India. William II became Kaiser of Germany that year. Czar Alexander III ruled Russia, and the Turkish Empire stretched from the Balkans to the tip of Arabia. To Westerners, the Far East was still a remote and mysterious land. Throughout the world, riding the back of an animal was the principal means of transportation. Unexplored and unmarked places dotted the global map.

On January 13, 1888, thirty-three men—scientists, cartographers, inventors, scholars, and explorers—met in Washington, D.C. They had accepted an invitation from Gardiner Greene Hubbard (1822–1897), the first president of the Bell Telephone Company and a leader in the education of the deaf, to form the National Geographic Society "to increase and diffuse geographic knowledge." One of the assembled group noted that they were the "first explorers of the Grand Canyon and the Yellowstone, those who had carried the American flag farthest north, who had measured the altitude of our famous mountains, traced the windings of our coasts and rivers, determined the distribution of flora and fauna, enlightened us in the customs of the aborigines, and marked out the path of storm and flood." Nine months later, the first issue of *National Geographic* magazine was sent out to 165 charter members. Today, more than a century later, membership has grown to an astounding 11 million in more than 170 nations. Several times that number regularly read the monthly issues of the *National Geographic* magazine.

The first years were difficult ones for the new magazine. The earliest volumes seem dreadfully scientific and quite dull. The articles in Volume I, No. 1 set the tone—W. M. Davis, "Geographic Methods in Geologic Investigation," followed by W. J. McGee, "The Classification of Geographic Forms by Genesis." Issues came out erratically—three in 1889, five in 1890, four in 1891, and two in 1895. In January 1896 "an illustrated monthly" was added to the title. The November issue that year contained a photograph of a half-naked Zulu bride and bridegroom in their wedding finery staring full face into the camera. But, a reader must have wondered what to make of the accompanying text: "These people . . . possess some excellent traits, but are horribly cruel when once they have smelled blood." In hopes of expanding circulation, the Board of Managers offered newsstand copies at $.25 each and began to accept advertising. But the magazine essentially remained unchanged. Circulation rose only slightly.

In January 1898, shortly after Gardiner Greene Hubbard's death, his son-in-law Alexander Graham Bell (1847–1922) agreed to succeed him as the second president of the National Geographic Society. Bell invented the telephone in 1876 and, while pursuing his lifelong goal of improving the lot of the deaf, had turned his amazingly versatile mind to contemplating such varied problems as human flight, air conditioning, and popularizing geography. The society then had about 1,100 members—the magazine was on the edge of bankruptcy. Bell did not want the job. He wrote in his diary, though, that he accepted leadership of the society "in order to save it." "Geography is a fascinating subject and it can be made interesting," he told the board of directors. Bell abandoned the unsuccessful attempt to increase circulation through newsstand sales. "Our journal," he wrote, "should go to members, people who believe in our work and want to help." He understood that the lure for prospective members should be an association with a society that made it possible for the average person to share with kings and scientists the excitement of sending an expedition to a strange land or an explorer to an inaccessible region. This idea, more than any other, has been responsible for the growth of the National Geographic Society and for the popularity of the magazine. "I can well remember," recalled Bell in 1912, "how the idea was laughed at that we should ever reach a membership of ten thousand." That year it had soared to 107,000!

Bell attributed this phenomenal growth, though, to one man who had transformed the *National Geographic* magazine into "the greatest educational journal in the world"—Gilbert H. Grosvenor (1875–1966). Bell had hired Grosvenor, then 24, in 1899 as the National Geographic Society's first full-time employee, "to put some life into the magazine." He personally escorted the new editor, who would become his son-in-law, to the society's headquarters—a small rented room shared with the American Forestry Association on the fifth floor of a building near the U.S. Treasury in downtown Washington. Grosvenor remembered the headquarters "littered with old magazines, newspapers, and a few record books and six enormous boxes crammed with *Geographics* returned by the newsstands." "No desk!" exclaimed Bell. "I'll send you mine." That afternoon, delivery men brought Grosvenor a large walnut rolltop and the new editor began to implement Bell's instructions—to transform the magazine from one of cold geographic fact "expressed in hieroglyphic terms which the layman could not understand into a vehicle for carrying the living, breathing, human-interest truth about this great world of ours to the people." And what did Bell consider appropriate "geographic subjects"? He replied: "The world and all that is in it is our theme."

Grosvenor shared Bell's vision of a great society and magazine that would disseminate geographic knowledge. "I thought of geography in terms of its Greek root: *geographia*—a description of the world," he later wrote. "It thus becomes the most catholic of subjects, universal in appeal, and embracing nations, people, plants, birds, fish. We would never lack interesting subjects." To attract readers, Grosvenor had to change the public attitude toward geography, which he knew was regarded as "one of the dullest of all subjects, something to inflict upon schoolboys and avoid in later life." He wondered why certain books that relied heavily on geographic description remained popular—Charles Darwin's *Voyage of the Beagle*, Richard Dana Jr.'s *Two Years Before the Mast*, and even Herodotus's *History*. Why did readers for generations—and with Herodotus's travels, for 20 centuries—return to these books? What did these volumes, which used so many geographic descriptions, have in common? What was the secret? According to Grosvenor, the answer was that "each was an accurate, eyewitness, firsthand account. Each contained simple straightforward writing—writing that sought to make pictures in the reader's mind."

Gilbert Grosvenor was editor of the *National Geographic* magazine for 55 years, from 1899 until 1954. Each of the 660 issues under his direction had been a highly readable geography textbook. He took Bell's vision and made it a reality. Acclaimed as "Mr. Geography," he discovered the earth anew for himself and for millions around the globe. He charted the dynamic course that the National Geographic Society and its magazine followed for more than half a century. In so doing, he forged an instrument for world education and understanding unique in this or any age. Under his direction, the *National Geographic* magazine grew in circulation from a few hundred copies—he recalled carrying them to the post office on his back—to more than five million at the time of his retirement as editor, enough for a stack 25 miles high.

This Chelsea House series celebrates Grosvenor's first 25 years as editor of the *National Geographic*. "The mind must see before it can believe," said Grosvenor. From the earliest days, he filled the magazine with photographs and established another Geographic principle—to portray people in their natural attire or lack of it. Within his own editorial committee, young Grosvenor encountered the prejudice that photographs had to be "scientific." Too often, this meant dullness. To Grosvenor, every picture and sentence had to be interesting to the layperson. "How could you educate and inform if you lost your audience by boring your readers?" Grosvenor would ask his staff. He persisted and succeeded in making the *National Geographic* magazine reflect this fascinating world.

To the young-in-heart of every age there is magic in the name *National Geographic*. The very words conjure up enchanting images of faraway places, explorers and scientists, sparkling seas and dazzling mountain peaks, strange plants, animals, people, and customs. The small society founded in 1888 "for the increase and diffusion of geographic knowledge" grew, under the guidance of one man, to become a great force for knowledge and understanding. This achievement lies in the genius of Gilbert H. Grosvenor, the architect and master builder of the National Geographic Society and its magazine.

Fred L. Israel
The City College of the City University of New York

REDISCOVERING ANCIENT EGYPT

Fred L. Israel

For thousands of years, Egyptians have lived along the banks of the Nile River. As Egypt is said to be the "gift of the Nile," so have the people been molded by the influences of the river. No country in the world is so dependent on a river that traverses it as Egypt, and no river presents such physical characteristics as exceptional as the Nile.

There is no culture in the world whose history is traceable to so remote a period as that of the Egyptians. Other peoples may have understood the art of writing as early as the Egyptians did, but no specimens of it have been preserved. Egyptian records, hewn in stone, burned in clay, written on leather or on scrolls of papyrus, have survived the ravages of thousands of years. The preservation of these materials is due mainly to the dryness of the air in the rainless Nile Valley and to the hot sands that hermetically seal everything committed to its keeping.

Written Egyptian documents date back to c. 3000 B.C., when the first pharaohs developed the hieroglyphic script. The documents of these kings and their successors, as well as the material aspects of their culture, were well preserved by this arid climate. Hieroglyphic documents plus archaeological remains are the primary sources for studying the fascinating history of this ancient people.

Probably more books and articles have been written about ancient Egypt than about any other field of archaeological investigation. Since 1901, *National Geographic* alone has published more than 25 major studies and each uniformly found an insatiable audience. The first, "Recent Discoveries in Egypt," began a trend that has lasted throughout the century—of giving readers the latest information concerning fresh treasures from Egypt's sands.

Many *National Geographic* articles rank as seminal. For example, in 1911, Franklin Hoskins used archaeological evidence to trace the possible route over which Moses may have led the children of Israel out of Egypt. In 1923, a *Geographic* staff correspondent attended the official ceremonial opening of the tomb of King Tutankhamen (c. 1361–1352 B.C.). His account appeared in a 1924 issue. Forty-five years later, a *National Geographic* research grant financed a computer program to re-create images of Egyptian temples (see November 1970 issue). And in January 1988, the magazine reported the discovery—and printed the first photographs—of a 4,600-year old boat entombed in a pit beside the Great Pyramid of Khufu at Giza.

Ancient Egypt has a wealth of monuments—tombs, temples, palaces, dwellings, and military sites—that scholars use to re-create some 6,000 years of civilization. The dry climate essential for preservation, together with the Egyptian custom of burying their dead surrounded by objects for use in the next life, has ensured an abundance of well-preserved material. The direct consequence of this custom—the pillaging of tombs—was to become a national pastime and was a fate few tombs escaped. Ancient Egypt also had an extensive bureaucracy that kept detailed records of legal matters and historical events. Likewise, Egyptians customarily decorated their tombs and temples with stories and poetry. This rich legacy has provided an unsurpassed record of an ancient civilization.

In May 1798, some 10,000 sailors and 36,000 soldiers set sail from France to invade Egypt. Accompanying them was a team of mathematicians, astronomers, engineers, naturalists, and scientists of every description. For two years, they studied everything from the quality of the Nile River water to the possibility of linking the Mediterranean Sea with the Red Sea—the future Suez Canal. However, their principal interest was Egypt's past. The result was *Description of Egypt* (1809–1828), a massive 20-volume scholarly study. This work dates the beginning of the modern science of Egyptology.

In the first article of this compilation, James Baikie explains what the world has learned about ancient Egypt from the publication of *Description of Egypt* through the first decade of the 20th century. It is an outstanding article. Baikie captures the everyday life, explaining how every scrap of information, from temple inscriptions to lists of rulers, although damaged and often incomplete, must be fitted patiently into a complicated mosaic.

The two articles that follow summarize work undertaken by the Egyptian Exploration Fund, a private organization devoted to furthering knowledge through the financing of excavations.

Vol. XXIV, No. 9   WASHINGTON   September, 1913

THE RESURRECTION OF ANCIENT EGYPT

By James Baikie
Author of "Sea Kings of Crete," in
the National Geographic Magazine, January, 1912

IF THE Elizabethan age was the period of the discovery of new worlds, a period bright with all the romance and fascination of man's adventure into the unknown, our own age may be defined as the period of the resurrection of ancient worlds, and the romance of the explorations which have given back to us the buried civilizations of Assyria, Babylonia, Egypt, Crete, and Asia Minor has in its own way been almost as thrilling as that which marked the discoveries of Columbus, Cortez, and Pizarro. Ancient and mighty empires, which lived for us only in the dim traditions and distorted pictures of classical historians, have risen out of the dust of the past.

They have begun to take shape and solidity before our eyes; their palaces, their temples, and their tombs have yielded us unquestionable and vivid illustration of the height of culture which they had reached in almost incredibly ancient days. It is scarcely an exaggeration to say that we know as much of the life and the customs of the leading peoples of four millenniums ago as we do of those of the European nations of the Middle Ages.

In the wonderful record of exploration which has restored to us the civilization of the great pre-classical nations, there is no more remarkable chapter than that which tells of the resurrection of ancient Egypt. It contains perhaps no incident so thrilling as Layard's discovery of the buried palaces of Assyria, or Evans's unearthing the legendary Labyrinth of Minos in Crete, for the mightiest relics of the power of ancient Egypt—the Pyramids, the Colossi, the temples of Karnak and Luxor—have never ceased through all the centuries to bear their evidence to the greatness of the men who reared them. But it is only within the lifetime of the present generation that exploration of the wonders of which these were the surface indications has become systematic, and that we have begun to pass from the stage of mere wonder to that of scientific research and coördination of the facts disclosed by excavation.

The science of Egyptology, which is slowly and patiently reconstructing for us the ordered history of the 3,000 years before Christ, and enabling us to see the types of men, the manner of life, the forms of government, the religious customs and beliefs of period after period, from the very dawn of Egyptian nationality, is specifically a growth of our own time.

ROUGH AND READY METHODS OF EARLY EXPLORERS

The older period of Egyptian exploration may be said to have closed with Mariette. Despite his abundant energy, his wonderful instinct for a promising site, and the astonishing amount of interesting material which he accumulated during his explorations, this devoted explorer had not the genius of patience and orderliness, the sense of relation, and the conviction of the importance of all facts and things, however small, which characterize the modern scientific spirit. His undeniably important work was done in a big, broad, and also somewhat loose and wasteful fashion; and while we can see and acknowledge how much he discovered and preserved, we can only conjecture how much was overlaid and lost in the process.

The meshes of his wide-flung net were too large to deal with the smaller spoil of the archeologist, and he could not understand that from the point of view of knowledge to be gained from it a potsherd may be more important than a pyramid. Modern investigation no longer proceeds on his somewhat slapdash and wasteful methods. It holds no site to have been really explored till every scrap of pottery which it yields has been collected, numbered, and studied, and the very earth and sand have been painfully riddled through a sieve.

The result of all this laborious investigation is that instead of being confronted with a confused mass of facts, wonderful enough individually, but unrelated and perplexing, we are gradually being presented with a coherent picture of the history and the life of the various periods of tile ancient Egyptian nationality from its earliest days down to historic times.

Modern exploration has not, of course followed and could not follow a strictly chronological order in its researches. Explorers had to take and to interpret whatever a site yielded to them, whether it belonged to the first dynasty or the thirtieth, or to both. As a matter of fact, perhaps the greatest impulse was given, as certainly the greatest popular interest was excited, by a discovery whose fruits belong largely to what must be considered a comparatively late period of Egyptian history—the discovery of the cache of royal mummies at Deir-el-Bahari.

But our purpose will best be served by disregarding the order of time in which the discoveries have been made and tracing the growth of modern knowledge concerning the various historical periods, beginning with the earliest dynasties.

THE HISTORY OF MANETHO VERIFIED

We owe the framework into which we try to fit the facts of Egyptian history to the ancient historian, Manetho, scattered fragments of whose history of Egypt, dating from the reign of Ptolemy Philadelphus, in the third century B.C., have come down to us in the works of various ancient authors. He recognized thirty dynasties of Egyptian monarchs, and he has left lists of the names of the kings in each of these dynasties, together with

THE FIRST ATTEMPT AT A PYRAMID: SAQQARA, EGYPT

According to the Greek historian, Manetho, this was the first stone building in the world. It was built by the architect Imhotep as a burial place for his master Zeser or Neterkhet, a king of the third dynasty. On the east and west sides the base measures 396 feet, the other two sides being 352 feet, while the height is about 195 feet. The chambers and passages within this step-pyramid are lined with blue and green glazed tiles, which bear the king's name and titles. This building represents the transition between the so-called "Mastaba" tombs in which the earlier kings were buried and the true pyramid of later date.

occasional notes upon matters of historical interest in particular reigns.

It has long been known that, whatever problems and difficulties might be connected with Manetho's later king lists (and these difficulties are neither few nor small), we at least began to get into touch with actual historic realities at the point where his fourth dynasty commences; for it was recognized that in his Souphis, Saphis, and Mencheres we had corruptions of the names of Khufu, Khafra, and Menkaura, the builders of the three largest pyramids (see pages 5, 6, 8, 10, and 11).

Beyond that point, however, history seemed to vanish into the mists. The kings of the earlier dynasties, Menes and the rest of them, were shadowy, unreal figures, who perhaps never existed save in the imagination of the historian—mere creatures of legend, such as we find at the beginning of all national histories. But if there has been one thing which modern investigation has taught us clearly, it is that the legends which describe the beginnings of national history are never mere figments of the imagination.

The generation which has seen the Labyrinth of Minos and the dancing-ground of Ariadne rise from the earth at Knossos may be held to have learned that lesson once for all. The people of the world's childhood were less imaginative and more truthful than we had supposed, and a legend on the surface of history means a historical fact buried somewhere beneath if only you can unearth it.

THE SEMI-MYTHICAL KINGS PROVE TO BE REAL

So it has proved to be with these shadowy kings of the earliest Egyptian dynasties. Manetho's fables about one of them being slain by a hippopotamus, while in the reign of another the Nile flowed with honey, may be mere fables; but the men were there, and their royalty was a very real and tangible thing. Since the early 1890s investigations have been carried out by de Morgan at Naqada and elsewhere, and by Amélineau, and especially by Petrie at Abydos, which have resulted in the discovery of the tombs of many of these ancient royalties and the accumulation of a most interesting mass of information with regard to the civilization of their time, the organization of their courts, and the attainments of the race over which they ruled.

The tombs of these ancient monarchs were not such as could be erected by a race undeveloped or just emerging from barbarism; they could only have been the product of a people comparatively far advanced in culture, and their contents revealed evidence not only of an astonishing proficiency in the arts of peace, but also of an elaborate and complex social organization, such as we should scarcely have deemed possible at so early a date.

The kings of the earliest dynasties reared no pyramids. Their tombs were great structures mainly underground—that of Aha (who is possibly Mena, the first king of Egypt) at Naqada measures 175 feet by 88 and contains 21 chambers—built sometimes of brick, with a lining of wood, and sometimes floored with stone, as in the case of the tomb of King Den at Abydos, whose granite floor furnishes the earliest known example of the use of stone in building.

These huge homes of the dead were filled with all sorts of objects which might be necessary or useful for the deceased king in the underworld.

THE KING'S SLAVES WERE SLAIN AT HIS GRAVE TO ACCOMPANY AND SERVE HIM IN THE AFTER-LIFE

Around him were buried his slaves, who were doubtless slain at his grave that they

AN EVENING VIEW OF THE PYRAMIDS, AS SEEN FROM THE VILLAGE OF KAFR

The little Arab village of Kafr is the nearest inhabited point to the pyramids of Gizeh, which stand on the yellow-brown sands of the vast Libyan desert, which stretches away to the west until it merges into the Sahara. These wonderful monuments are the property of a tribe of desert Arabs, who levy a toll (now fixed by the government) on all who come to view them. They lie on the west bank of the Nile about 5 miles southwest of Cairo, with which they are connected by a tramway.

might accompany and serve him in the afterlife. The chambers of his tomb were stored with stacks of great vases of wine and corn, with pottery dishes, splendid copper bowls, carved ivory boxes, golden buttons, palettes for grinding face paint, chairs and couches of elaborate design and decoration, ivory and pottery figurines, and plaques bearing records of the king's valor in war or his piety in the founding of temples.

Here and there in this wreckage of immemorial splendors a little touch helps us to realize that these dim historic figures were real men, who loved and sorrowed as men do still. Close to Mena's second tomb at Abydos lies that of his daughter—Bener-ab, "Sweetheart," as he called her—to suggest how love and death went side by side then as now.

The furniture of the tombs reveals an amazing proficiency in the arts and crafts. Ebony chests inlaid with ivory, stools with ivory feet carved in the shape of bull's legs, vessels cut and ground to translucent thinness, not only out of soft alabaster, but out of an iron-hard

PRAYER ON THE GREAT DESERT,
UNDER THE SHADOW OF THE THREE PYRAMIDS OF GIZEH

These most famous of all the pyramids of Egypt were built as tombs for three kings of the fourth dynasty. At the extreme right of the picture stands the Great Pyramid, the tomb of Khufu or Cheops; next to it, in the center, is the Second Pyramid, or that of Khafra; while to the left is the Third or smallest pyramid, that of Menkaura. The height of the Second Pyramid is only a few feet less than that of Khufu, but it stands on a platform of rock, which gives it the appearance of being higher than it really is. Menkaura's pyramid is less than half the height of the others and is inferior both in dimensions and workmanship. The sarcophagus of the king was discovered in it in 1838, but was unfortunately lost at sea while being shipped to England.

stone like diorite, finely wrought copper ewers, all tell us that the Egyptian of the earliest dynastic period was no rude barbarian, but a highly civilized craftsman. Perhaps the daintiest and most convincing evidence of his skill is given by the bracelets which were found encircling the

skeleton arm of the queen of King Zer, of the first dynasty, which, alike for the grace of their design and for the skill with which the gold is wrought and soldered, are admirable.

But these tombs have not only yielded evidence of the skill of the Egyptian workman;

THE SPHINX

Near the Second Pyramid stands the Sphinx, the most famous and mysterious of all Egyptian sculptures. This huge human-headed lion lies half buried in the sand looking due east across the Nile. The body is 150 feet long, the paws are 50 feet, and from the base to the top of the head the height is 70 feet. No one knows when this royal portrait was erected, but it seems probable that it was at some period during the fourth dynasty. Between its paws is a tablet relating how Tahutmes IV, a king of the 18th dynasty, found the statue buried in the sand and how, in a response to a vision, he excavated it. Rameses II, the Ptolemies, and the Romans restored broken parts, and at the last clearing of the sand portions of the beard were found between the paws. The name of the Sphinx in Egyptian was Hu.

they have taught us that even at this incredibly early date the nation had a complete method of expressing its thought and had reached a thoroughness of organization which we should not have imagined possible. At an early period in the first dynasty hieroglyphic writing has begun to make its appearance; by the middle of the period it is completely developed; before the end of the dynasty it has already become so familiar that the symbols are carelessly engraved. On the very lowest date which may be assigned to the dynasty this fact gives the Egyptian an astounding start of all other nations in the art of writing.

The inscriptions tell us of a court fully organized, with a complete bureaucracy. Mena has his chamberlain. His successor, Zer, tells us of a "commander of the inundation" a proof of

THE SECOND PYRAMID

The Second Pyramid, the tomb of Khafra, is not of such perfect workmanship as the Great Pyramid, though it is in some respects better preserved. All three pyramids were originally sheathed from base to summit in magnificent casings of limestone, which were so skillfully laid and finished that it was almost impossible to discern the joints. These casings remained intact until the 13th century of our era, when the Moslem builders of Cairo despoiled the pyramids to obtain material for the mosques and palaces of their city. All that now remains is at the apex of the Second Pyramid, as can be seen in the picture. This masonry cap extends for 150 feet and furnishes an excellent scale by which some idea of the vast mass of this great monument may be obtained.

the early date at which the Nile flood was utilized and regulated for the benefit of the land. In subsequent reigns of the same dynasty we meet with a "commander of the elders," a "keeper of the wine" (the earliest ancestor of the "Pharaoh's chief butler," with whom we have so long been familiar), a "leader of the peers," head of the most ancient of earthly aristocracies, and a "master of ceremonies," while the titles of "royal seal bearer," "scribe of accounts of provisions," "keeper of the king's vineyards," and "royal architect" show us with what minuteness the business affairs of the court were regulated.

THE CIVILIZATION OF EGYPT A SLOW GROWTH

In a sense these revelations of the earliest Egyptian dynastic civilization have done much to simplify the enigma presented by Egyptian history. The civilization of the Nile Valley no longer challenges us with the Great Pyramid as the first essay of its development or seems to spring full-grown like Athene from the head of Zeus.

We can see that civilization in Egypt followed the natural course of development by which it has grown to maturity in all other lands. It was the gradual growth of many centuries of patient effort on the part of pioneers whose greatness the later Egyptians reverenced by a true instinct, though perhaps their actual knowledge of them was even scantier than that which the excavations of Abydos have given to us.

In another sense, however, the wonder has only been increased by the disclosure of the fact that the rise and development of this race are so much more ancient than was believed a few years ago to be the case. The emergence from the mists of the past of this ancient world, with its great kings, its ordered courts, and its highly organized government, is surely one of the most dramatic surprises which the progress of scientific investigation has presented to the modern mind.

AT WHAT DATE DOES HISTORY DAWN IN EGYPT?

To what date are we to assign these earliest beginnings of monarchy? Here, unfortunately, we become at once involved in a controversy in which a century is but "as yesterday when it is past, and as a watch in the night." Egyptology is at present hopelessly divided against itself over the question of all dates prior to 1580 B.C. Into the details of the controversy it is useless to dream of entering.

Between the dating of the Berlin school, represented by Mayer, Erman, and Breasted of Chicago, and the longer system, whose chief

advocate is Flinders Petrie, there is a systematic difference of many centuries. Petrie places the beginnings of the first dynasty at 5510 B.C., while the Berlin school brings them down to 3400 B.C.

The difference is staggering and no compromise upon a middle term is possible; only the emergence of fresh facts can settle the question. At present the balance of opinion inclines toward the shorter system of dates; yet it must be remembered that new discoveries may at any moment make it untenable and force us back upon Professor Petrie's ampler scheme. In any case, and upon the most conservative estimate, we must accept the fact that by the middle of the fourth millennium B.C. society in Egypt was already in a state of high organization and culture.

Thus the discoveries of the last few years, and especially those of Professor Petrie at Abydos, have put our ideas of these earliest dynasties of Egypt upon a solid basis of material fact. The interpretation of the results and the identification of the various kings whose relics have been discovered are slow and laborious processes, involving much controversy; but the uncertainty of many of the details does not affect the outstanding historical fact. The kings existed and ruled over a state which, far from being barbarous, was already far advanced in the scale of civilization.

AN HISTORIAN'S REPUTATION RESTORED BY A MUMMY

That these early centuries witnessed a steady growth in knowledge and power on the part of the rulers of the Nile Valley is evidenced by the explorations which have been made with regard to the kings of the dynasties immediately succeeding. In 1900 Garstang excavated at Bet-Khallaf, near Abydos, the tombs of two of

A NEAR VIEW OF THE GREAT PYRAMID

No building, ancient or modern, has ever commanded so much interest and attention as this vast tomb of Khufu. Today it measures about 755 feet at the base and its height is 451 feet. Before its outer limestone casing was removed the sides were 20 feet longer and the top 30 feet higher. It has been calculated that the weight of its stones amounts to some 6 million tons and that it contains enough material to build a town large enough to house 120,000 people. The Greek historian, Herodotus, states that 100,000 men were employed for over 20 years in its erection, working in relays of three months at a time. Near the Second Pyramid the remains of barracks, affording accommodation for 4,000 skilled masons, can still he traced. The stone was cut from quarries on the opposite side of the Nile and floated across at the time of the annual inundation.

ASCENDING THE GREAT PYRAMID

"Accuracy equal to optician's work, but on a scale of acres instead of inches, is scarcely what one expects in buildings reared nearly 5,000 years ago, but the huge blocks of the Great Pyramid, 2,300,000 of them, weighing on an average of 2½ tons apiece, while some run to 40 and 50 tons, are squared, fitted, and leveled with an accuracy which puts to shame our best modern work, and compels our respect not only for the strength, but for the skill, of these mighty builders before the Lord" (see page 17).

LOOKING DOWN THE MAIN PASSAGE LEADING TO
KHUFU'S SEPULCHER WITHIN THE GREAT PYRAMID

Right in the heart of the Great Pyramid was the sepulchral chamber of Khufu (Cheops), approached by this gloomy passage. It is 175 feet long and 28 feet high, but only 7 feet in width. The four natives with candles give some idea of its length and gloom, the last candle showing as a mere spot of light glimmering in the distance. Notice the perfection with which the stones join each other, especially at the right of the picture. Some of these blocks, weighing many tons, are set together with a contact of one five-hundreths of an inch, a refinement of the mason's art which is seldom or never equaled in our own day.

BROKEN BY ROBBERS: KHUFU'S SARCOPHAGUS,
IN THE SEPULCHER CHAMBER OF THE GREAT PYRAMID, EGYPT

Unlike the rest of the pyramid, which is faced with limestone, the burial chamber of Khufu is constructed of great blocks of weathered granite cut from the rocks at the first cataract of the Nile. Over it are five small chambers, one above the other, designed to render the roof of the burial chamber safe by relieving it of some of the weight of the vast mass, which would otherwise press dangerously upon it. After the body of Khufu was laid in his great sarcophagus, the entrance to this chamber was sealed and workmen dropped into their places great blocks of granite, filling the end of the passage for 17 feet; then a cunningly devised block was filled into the entrance which hid all appearances of an opening. Yet, despite all these precautions, the rest of the great King was disturbed by Arab tomb robbers, who forced their way in, plundered the sacred body, and carried off the jewels and the rich furniture which always surrounded the royal dead.

ENTRANCE TO THE TOMBS QF THE SACRED BULLS AT SAQQARA
The tunneling goes far under the desert. There are 24 huge marble sarcophagi, each dedicated to one of the sacred bulls.

the earliest kings of the third dynasty—Zeser and Sa-nekht. The tomb of Zeser is a huge mass of brickwork 300 feet in length by 150 in breadth and 40 in height. The actual tomb chambers are hewn in the rock 20 feet below the ground level and 60 feet below that of the summit of the tomb.

Unfortunately, like so many of the royal tombs of Egypt, the great sepulcher had been rifled in ancient days; but sufficient relics survived, in the shape of clay jar-sealings, alabaster vases and bowls, and other articles, to identify the owner of the tomb. Sa-nekht's tomb was very similar to Zeser's, and the skeleton of the dead king, which was found in it, seems to suggest that poor Manetho, whose credit as an accurate historian has often suffered at the hands of incredulous moderns, was not always so inaccurate as he has been accused of being.

Among the marvels which he relates of the early kings there is a statement that a certain king named Sesokhris measured 5 cubits in height. The skeleton of Sa-nekht proves its owner to have been a giant 7 feet high, and it is tempting to identify him with Manetho's five-cubit Sesokhris, especially as names were never Manetho's strong point.

THE BUILDERS OF THE PYRAMIDS

Like many of these ancient kings, Zeser was not content with a single tomb. He had another at Saqqara, near Memphis—well known to Egyptian tourists as the Step Pyramid—the most imposing structure which has survived from such an early date. It measures between 300 and 400 feet in length on the sides

GOING TO BED IN A CUP

These curious cup-like structures, made of sun-baked mud, are seen in Egyptian villages. Families sleep in them at night during the great heat of the summer to escape the snakes and scorpions which abound.

and is 195 feet in height, while the chambers of the interior were lined with fine blue and green glazed tiles (see page 3).

A king who could rear such a structure had evidently at command the resources of a very well organized state and capable architects.

Zeser's architect and vizier, Imhotep, became in later days the typical wise man of Egypt, "whose counsel was as though one inquired at the oracle of God." He was the patron saint of the Egyptian scribe, who always poured a libation to him from his water-jar before beginning to write.

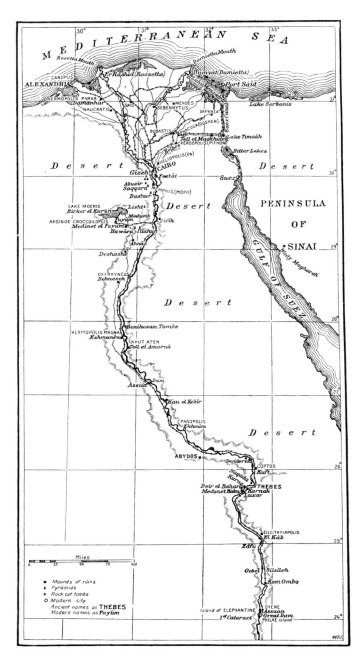

THE NILE FROM ITS MOUTH TO THE FIRST CATARACT

Two thousand five hundred years after his death he had been transformed into a god of medicine, whom the Greeks knew as Imouthis and whom they identified with their own Asklepios.

The head of the giant Sa-nekht, carved in the rock of the Wady Maghareh at Sinai, presents strongly marked Ethiopian characteristics, and Petrie infers that the third dynasty marks an infusion of Ethiopian blood into the ruling race, whether by conquest or marriage, the mixture of race giving rise to the remarkable development of energy which characterized the succeeding dynasty.

That development, of course, is signalized by the achievements of the great fourth dynasty—the race of the pyramid builders. Modern investigation has added nothing very striking or novel to our knowledge of the mighty men who reared the greatest masses of stone ever heaped upon earth by the hand of man; but Petrie's course of systematic triangulation and measurement, carried out in 1881-1882, has only added to the wonder and admiration which the mere aspect of the pyramids compel.

Accuracy "equal to optician's work, but on a scale of acres instead of inches," is scarcely what one expects in buildings reared nearly 5,000 years ago. But the huge blocks of the Great Pyramid, 2,300,000 of them, weighing on an average 2½ tons apiece, while some run to 40 and 50 tons, are squared, fitted, and leveled with an accuracy which puts to shame our best modern work and compels our respect not only for the strength, but for the skill of these mighty builders before the Lord (see pages 10 and 11).

No amount of mere brute strength could have accomplished such a feat. There must have been controlling intellect of the very highest type at work, supplemented by a determined and despotic will capable of bending the whole resources of the nation to a single task. That the task may have had as its sole object the glorifying of the egotism of a single individual need not diminish our wonder at the patience and skill with which it was carried out.

The most interesting result of modern investigation on this period of Egyptian history has, however, been one not of exploration, but of historical and literary work. An Egyptian papyrus of the twelfth dynasty, brought home by an English traveler, was transferred by its owner, Miss Westcar, to the famous German Egyptologist, Lepsius, from whose property it was purchased by the Berlin Museum. The Westcar papyrus has afforded us the earliest series of wonder tales known to exist in the world; but it has also yielded the hint of a sudden revolution in Egyptian history, and of the usurpation of the throne at the close of the great period of the pyramid builders by a line of priestly kings.

THE ARABIAN NIGHTS OF ANCIENT EGYPT

The story pictures to us King Khufu, the builder of the Great Pyramid, listening to his sons as they tell him tales of the great magicians of former days.

One of them, Prince Hordadef, tells him of a magician of the present time who can do deeds as great as those of any wonder-worker of the past. He is dispatched to summon the wizard, and, after the latter has given evidence of his power, he prophesies to the king of the approaching birth of three sons of a priest of the sun-god Ra, who shall be really children of the god and shall reign over the whole land of

TOMBS OF THE KINGS: THEBES

"In 1881 M. (now Sir Gaston) Maspero was led to the mouth of a disused tomb at the foot of the cliffs of Deir-el-Bahari, where, in the bowels of the earth, was discovered the most wonderful collection of the mummies of the great kings of the most glittering period of Egyptian history. . . . The mummies were found, by hastily scrawled inscriptions on their bandages, to have been gathered in their hiding place by the priests of the 21st and 22nd dynasties. . . . The panic-stricken priests shifted the bodies of their dead masters from tomb to tomb . . . until at last, about 940 B.C., they found in the pit of Deir-el-Bahari a resting place sufficiently obscure to baffle their relentless enemies" (see pages 32 and 35).

Egypt. The king is naturally troubled at such a prophecy, and the magician consoles him by telling him that the change of dynasty shall not come in his day. "Thy son, his son, and then one of these." The story then goes on to tell of the birth of these wonderful children and of the divine honors which attend them. Obviously we have here an attempt to give a popular account of the rise of a new race of kings devoted to the worship of Ra, the sun-god.

THE NEXT (FIFTH) DYNASTY WERE SUN-WORSHIPPERS

The complement of the narrative has been furnished by the excavations of the German explorers at Abusir, which have yielded unmistakable evidence of the fact that the kings of the fourth dynasty were succeeded by a dynasty of sun-worshipers. Von Bissing, Schaefer, Thiersch, Rubensohn, and Borchardt have there laid bare the great sun temple of Neuser-ra, sixth king of the fifth dynasty.

Its whole plan and conception are unlike those of the normal Egyptian temple. It consists of a large, open court, with chambers surrounding it; in the center of the court stands a huge altar of fine alabaster, on which slain oxen were offered to the sun, west of the altar rises a large mound, on which was placed a truncated obelisk—the emblem of the solar deity. There was no holy of holies, the emblem of the god standing open to the sky to catch the sun's rays.

The interior walls of the court were covered with reliefs representing the production of life, scenes from the river, swamps, fields, and incidents in the state worship, while on the outer walls were pictures of the warlike achievements of the Pharaoh. Beyond the court, on the south side, lay a great model of the bark of the sun-god, 96 feet long, built of

brick. Apparently each king of the dynasty erected such a temple, as a complete series can be traced, extending to the reign of Assa, the eighth king.

A RACE OF EXPLORERS AND ADVENTUROUS TRADERS

The kings of this line are also the first to begin systematic exploration of the surrounding countries. Already, a century and a half before, Seneferu, the last king of the third dynasty, had sent a fleet to Syria; but Sahura, the second king of the priestly line, records a voyage to Punt, or Somaliland, which resulted in the bringing back of 80,000 measures of myrrh, 6,000 pounds weight of electrum (gold-silver alloy), and 2,000 staves of ebony wood. Assa, one of Sahura's successors, began that exploration of the Sudan which was continued so vigorously by the barons of Elephantine under the kings of the next dynasty. Altogether the priestly line of Heliopolis seems to have been more vigorous than priestly lines have usually been in the experience of other nations.

Perhaps the most remarkable result of investigation into the story of Egypt during the period covered by the next line of kings with whom the Old Kingdom, as it is named, closes is the proof afforded by the records that our old idea of Egypt, as a kind of China of ancient days, strictly isolated from other nations and jealous of all communication with them, must be entirely discarded. Far from being a secluded people, the Egyptains, even at this early period of their history, were active and enterprising merchants and explorers, pushing their trade far into the Sudan and maintaining regular communication by sea with Somaliland and Syria, and in all probability with the rising Minoan Empire of Crete.

USHABTIS, OR ANSWERERS

It was the custom with the earlier dynasties when a king died to slay all the members of his harem and many slaves, that they might be buried with him. Later, instead of human sacrifices, these little figures, or mimic servants, were substituted (see page 28).

THEY CAPTURE A PIGMY FOR THE KING

The story of the exploration of the Sudan and the Red Sea voyages we owe to the decipherment of the tomb inscriptions of the barons of Elephantine, who during the reigns of the sixth dynasty were the wardens of the Egyptian marches on the southern frontier—"Keepers of the Gate of the South"—as they called themselves. The most interesting of these inscriptions is that of Herkhuf, who tells us of four expeditions which he made into the Sudan for gold-dust and ivory. On the last of these he got into touch, as Assa's caravan leader had done before him, with a tribe of that race of pigmies whom Stanley encountered in his search for Emin Pasha. Herkhuf succeeded in capturing one of the dwarfs and bringing him back to Egypt in safety.

His king, Pepy II, who at this time was a boy of 8 years, was highly delighted at the news of the capture of so choice a plaything, and wrote Herkhuf a gracious letter of thanks, full of minute instructions as to the care to be exercised over his precious charge. Herkhuf is to take great precautions lest the dwarf should fall into the river on his way down the Nile, and proper people are to watch behind the place where he sleeps, and to look into his bed ten times in the course of each night to see that all is well.

A QUAINT LETTER

"My Majesty," says the king, "wisheth to see this pigmy more shall all tribute of Bata and Punt. And if thou comest to court having this pigmy with thee sound and whole, My Majesty will do for thee more than was done for the divine Chancellor Baurdeed in the times of King Assa, and conformably to the greatness of the desire of the heart of My Majesty to see this pigmy." Herkhuf was so proud of the king's letter that he caused it to be engraved, word for word, on the wall of his tomb at Elephantine as proof of the royal favor which he enjoyed.

It was in the small pyramids reared by the kings of this and the preceding dynasty, and mainly opened by Maspero in the early eighties, that there were found the so-called "Pyramid Texts," which have furnished us with most of our knowledge as to Egyptian religious beliefs in the earliest historical periods. These texts reveal an exceedingly primitive and almost savage set of religious conceptions, especially with regard to the life after death which contrasts somewhat strangely with the high standard of material civilization which the period had attained.

A wild fancy pictures the deceased king ascending to heaven as a fierce huntsman who lassoes the stars and devours the gods. "Heaven rains, the stars fight, the Bowmen [one of the constellations] wander about when they have seen how he ascends and has a soul as a god who lives upon his fathers and feeds upon his mothers. . . . He devours men and lives upon the gods. . . . He it is who devours their magic and swallows their illuminated ones. The great ones among them are his morning meal, the middle ones are his evening meal, and the small ones his night meal. . . . Their magic is in his body; he swallows the understanding of every god."

Such ideas are not uncommon among cannibal tribes at the present time; but they coexist somewhat strangely with all the material splendors of the Old Kingdom and with the placid common sense and genial worldly wisdom which have already begun to find literary expression in the precepts of Ptah-hotep and Gemnikai.

THE DARK AGES OF EGYPTIAN HISTORY

With the decline of the Old Kingdom, at the close of the sixth dynasty, we enter upon one of the great dark periods of Egyptian history, whose darkness even the industry of modern exploration has done very little to lighten—probably because there is very little to discover about the period. It seems to have been a time when the elements of society in the land were in a state of solution, when the central power of the old Memphite monarchy no longer sufficed to control the feudal barons and princelets, and when the strife for dominion between the northern and southern sections of the community prevented that settling down to peaceful industry without which great work cannot be done.

AN EGYPTIAN NOBLE AND HIS WIFE

This mural painting is in one of the rock-hewn tombs at Thebes, in the room where the deceased nobleman and his wife were supposed to live and eat the offering of food and drink supplied by their surviving relatives and friends. In the upper left-hand corner the whole family are depicted fowling and fishing. Like all the wall paintings in the Egyptian tombs, the colors are as fresh and vivid as if laid on yesterday, instead of more than 3,000 years ago.

QUEEN TYI

"Queen Tyi deserves to rank with Queen Hatshepsut as one of the two most remarkable women whom Egypt has produced. . . . In February, 1905, Mr. T. M. Davis . . . discovered the tomb of Yuaa and Thuaa, the father and mother of that Queen Tyi, whose influence played so great a part in Akhenaten's religious reformation. It had become almost an accepted belief that Tyi, whose influence was so pronouncedly pro-Mesopotamian, must have been herself of Mesopotamian origin. The tomb of Yuaa and Thuaa, however, reveal the fact that her parents were purely Egyptian, and . . . though probably not of royal rank, Queen Tyi's parents were at least people of considerable importance" (see pages 37 and 45).

MUMMIFIED MONKEYS AND DOG FOUND BY THEODORE M. DAVIS IN THE TOMB OF AMENHOTEP II

This king was very fond of monkeys, and when he died his pets were placed near him. The Egyptians seem to have mummified almost everything that had life; animals. birds, fishes, and insects were embalmed, and even the meat ceremonially offered to the dead was subjected to a similar process. Vast cemeteries of sacred animals and birds have been found, such as the great cat cemetery at Bubastis. In preserving the larger animals it was not the custom to embalm the entire body; thus, in the case of a cow, for example, it would be represented in the mummy by the head and a selection of the bones.

MORE MUMMIFIED MONKEYS FROM THE TOMB OF AMENHOTEP II

Other curious contents of the tombs were mummified ducks and chickens. These were preserved in wooden vessels, carved to represent the bird they contained. Another vessel contained delicious honey, which had been there for thousands of years.

The seventh, eighth, ninth, and tenth dynasties remain more or less shadowy to us, and we have only brief suggestions and glimpses of a civil strife which surged hither and thither in the narrow Nile Valley, as the princes of the north or the south alternately prevailed. The outcome of all the confusion was the shifting of the national center of gravity from Memphis to Thebes.

This took place under the eleventh dynasty, which may be dated about 3500 B.C. or 2160 B.C., according to the scheme of chronology which is preferred. The twelfth dynasty indeed shifted the seat of government again back to the neighborhood of the old northern capital; still they were Theban princes, and it is with Thebes that the story of Egypt's greatness is bound up during all the rest of her history.

One of the remarkable finds of modern excavation has been that of the great funerary temple of King Mentuhotep Neb-hapet-ra, of the eleventh dynasty, which has conclusively shown us that this line of kings, hitherto almost as shadowy as its immediate predecessors, was indeed a great and powerful dynasty, the worthy forerunner of the Amenemhats and Senuserts of the following line, who brought in the Golden Age of the Middle Kingdom.

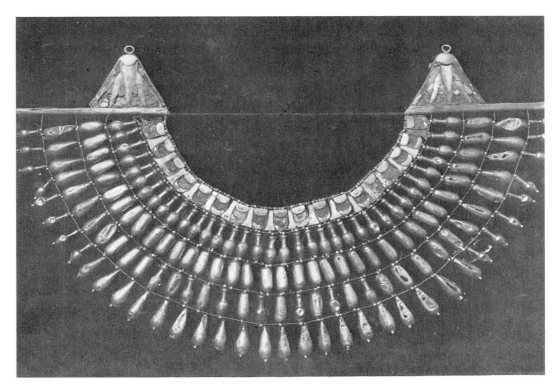

GOLD NECKLACE FOUND BY THEODORE M. DAVIS
IN THE TOMB OF QUEEN TYI, JANUARY, 1907

"Egyptian jewelry, which has been familiar enough in specimens of the work of later periods, has often been
open to the reproach of being somewhat heavy and overloaded in design, though admirable in execution; but
the diadems of these royal ladies are of the most exquisite lightness and grace, combined with a skill in workmanship which would do honor to the most cunning craftsman of the present day" (see page 30).

ONE OF THE MOST BEAUTIFUL
TEMPLES EXCAVATED

At Deir-el-Bahari, near Thebes, there lies
in a great bay of the limestone cliffs one of the
most famous and beautiful of Egyptian temples, the terraced temple of Queen Hatshepsut,
of the eighteenth dynasty. This wonderful
building has always been known to exist and
was completely excavated by Professor Naville
in the nineties of last century. But on the completion of the work in 1898 there still remained
a large tract to the south of Hatshepsut's temple
covered with mounds of débris and awaiting
exploration. Here, in 1903, Professor Naville
resumed work for the Egyptian Exploration
Fund. Excavation speedily revealed the existence of a temple of considerable importance,

COLOSSI OF MEMNON ON THE PLAIN OF THEBES, LUXOR: EGYPT

Each colossus is 69 feet in height, hewn from a solid block of Assouan granite, weighing some 1,000 tons. The measurements of the colossi are startling: length of ear, 3½ feet; index finger, 3½ feet; breadth of foot across toes, 4½ feet; area of nail, middle finger, 35 square inches. After an earthquake in 27 B.C. the colossus on the right was damaged and began to emit a cry every morning shortly after sunrise, and the Greek residents of Egypt immediately identified the statue as Memnon, son of Eos, the Dawn. Many visitors were attracted by this phenomenon, including, in 130 A.D., the Emperor Hadrian, who, following the immemorial habit of tourists, scratched his name at the base. This strange cry was due to the rapid expansion of the stone caused by the beat of the morning sun.

and the completion of the work laid bare the remains of a building fairly comparable in scale with the more famous temple beside it, anticipating to some extent the peculiar architectural features of the latter, hitherto supposed to be unique, and excelling the eighteenth dynasty building in solidity of workmanship.

On an artificially squared rectangular platform of natural rock about 15 feet high was reared the pyramid of the king—a dummy, for his tomb has not been found. Around the pyramid was an ambulatory, whose roof was supported by octagonal pillars, while its outside walls were decorated with scenes of religious festivals, processions, husbandry, and so forth. To north and south were open courts, and the faces of the rock platform were riveted with large blocks of white limestone, some of them measuring 6 feet by 3 feet 6 inches, beautifully squared and laid. A sloping ramp led up to the platform of the temple, and was bordered by colonnades of 22 pillars, each inscribed with the king's names and titles.

The royal tomb, as already mentioned, was not found; but all around the central pyramid priestesses of the goddess Hathor were buried in small chambertombs. They were all members of the king's harem, and were called "royal favorites." From the fact that they were all buried at one time before the completion of the temple, it has been inferred that they were strangled at the king's death that their spirits might accompany him into the underworld. If so (the inference is not certain by any means), then this is the last instance of the occurrence of so savage a custom.

Already these royal favorites have buried with them the little figures, *ushabtis*, or "answerers," upon which later Egyptians depended for service in the life beyond. Hence-

forward even royalty had to content itself with these mimic servants instead of the human *ushabtis* who had formerly been sacrificed to its importance (see page 20).

AN ARTIST'S AUTOBIOGRAPHY

Fortunately the name of the chief artist of Mentuhotep's reign has been preserved to us, with his description of his own qualifications. On a tombstone from Abydos, now in the Louvre, this great man, Mertisen by name, thus describes himself:

"I was an artist skilled in my art. I knew my art—how to represent the forms of going forth and returning, so that each limb might be in its proper place. I knew how the figure of a man should walk, and the carriage of a woman, the poising of the arm to bring the hippopotamus low, the going of the runner. I knew how to make amulets, which enable us to go without fire burning us and without the flood washing us away. No man could do this but I and the eldest son of my body. Him has the god decreed to excel in art, and I have seen the perfection of the work of his hands in every kind of rare stone, in gold and silver, in ivory and ebony."

In all probability it was this great and modest artist who planned Mentuhotep's temple, and, if so, we know the names of the builders of both the great temples at Deir-el-Bahari, for that of Hatshepsut was executed by Sen-mut, the queen's famous minister and architect.

The reasons which induced the Theban princes of the following dynasty to shift their court once more to the neighborhood of Memphis are unknown, though we may conjecture that the northern part of the kingdom, long accustomed to political supremacy, was proving restive under the transference of authority to

STATUE OF RAMESES II: MEMPHIS

Looking at this picture, it seems difficult to realize that these palm trees are growing in what were once the streets of the busy metropolis of ancient Egypt. As late as the Moslem conquest Memphis was still an important city, but after the twelfth century it began to serve as a quarry of building stone for the Arab cities of Fostat and Cairo, and so continued until all that is left is the solitary portrait statue of Rameses II, which once stood at the entrance of one of its temples. The statue is of granite brought from the quarries at the first cataract of the Nile, 600 miles away, and, excluding the crown, is 25 feet long.

the south. At all events the kings of the twelfth dynasty, who must rank among the greatest monarchs of the land, held their court at a fortified palace called Thet-taui, near the ancient Memphis, and much of the great work which they did for Egypt was accomplished in the neighborhood of the Fayum.

It was there that they were laid to rest in their brick pyramids, which have been explored, at various periods from 1888 onward, by Professor Petrie, M. de Morgan, and MM. Gautier and Jéquier. Had it not been for the evidence afforded by the results of these excavations, we should have been left without any adequate illustration of the greatness of the period, for the twelfth dynasty work has otherwise largely disappeared from the land.

The earliest excavation was that of the pyramid of Amenemhat III at Hawara. The pyramid itself yielded but little spoil. Its chief interest lay in the elaborate precautions which had been taken, by means of false passages and gigantic plug blocks of stone closing the true passages, to weary and defeat the efforts of tomb-robbers. Yet, in spite of all, it had been robbed in ancient days, not improbably with the connivance of the priests or officials in charge of the building, as only the outermost of the three great plug blocks closing the passages had ever been secured in its place.

But the amazing feature of the whole structure was the sepulchral chamber in which the royal sarcophagus had lain. No mere built chamber had been considered costly or safe enough for the remains of so great a monarch. A huge block of quartzite had been hollowed out into a chamber measuring inside 22 feet by 8, with walls 3 feet in thickness. A single block of the same stone formed a roof, the chamber itself weighing 110 tons and the roof 45.

The later Egyptians of the eighteenth and nineteenth dynasties handled, in the open, blocks much larger than this, the record being the seated colossus of Rameses II at Thebes, which weighed 1,000 tons (see page 51), but the skill and resource involved in the accurate placing of such a mass of stone in its confined situation inspire a wholesome respect for the Egyptian workman of the twelfth dynasty.

The pyramid of Senusert II at Dashur was excavated in 1894-1896 by M. de Morgan, with the assistance of MM. Legrain and Jéquier. The chief find of importance lay outside the pyramid, where some of the princesses of the royal house had been buried in a series of tombs opening out of a subterranean gallery.

Here were found the wonderful jewels of the princesses Sit-hathor and Merit, which have given us a new conception of the skill and taste of the Egyptian goldsmith.

Egyptian jewelry, which has been familiar enough in specimens of the work of later periods, has often been open to the reproach of being somewhat heavy and overloaded in design, though admirable in execution; but the diadems of these royal ladies are of the most exquisite lightness and grace, combined with a skill in workmanship which would do honor to the most cunning craftsman of the present day. Worthy to stand beside them are the great pectorals, or breast ornaments, bearing the names of Senusert II, Senusert III, and Amenemhat III, with their brilliant designs in cloisonné, where beautiful colored stones, lapis-lazuli, carnelian, and green feldspar take the place of enamels (compare page 26).

THE RESURRECTION OF AN ANCIENT COUNTRY TOWN

Totally devoid of beauty, but more valuable to us than the most beautiful works of art, was the discovery made by Petrie in 1889-1890 of the remains of the town of Kahun, close to the pyramid of Senusert II at Illahun. It was known that Senusert had established a town for the builders of his pyramid, naming it "Ha-hetep-Senusert," "Senusert is content."

Petrie's excavations revealed the beginnings of the town wall close to the north side of the pyramid, and street by street the whole was cleared, until the practically unchanged plan of an Egyptian working-class town of the twelfth dynasty was revealed. The workmen of those days were poorly lodged. Their low mud-brick thatched houses were crowded into congested groups, separated by narrow alleys, while there were great ranges of barrack-like structures with a multitude of small chambers under one roof, open passages affording access to the various rooms.

Even in these congested quarters, however, evidences were not wanting that the life of the inhabitants was on a higher plane than we should have imagined from the character of their homes. Various papyri, included among which were two wills, the earliest known instances of such documents, a hymn of praise to Senusert III, and some pages of a medical treatise, showed that letters were not unknown Toys of various kinds—whip-tops, model boats, dolls and draught-boards—suggested that child life has varied but little in its tastes through all the centuries.

HOW THE EGYPTIANS MADE FIRE

The question of how the Egyptians made fire was one that had often exercised archeologists. No representation of the process existed on the monuments, nor does the nation appear to have attached any religious significance to the origin of fire. The question was settled by the discovery at Kahun of a regular bow-drill for making fire, together with several sticks showing the burnt holes caused by fire-drilling. Mixed with remains of twelfth dynasty Egyptian pottery were fragments of vessels which we now know to be of unmistakable Ægean fabric. Thus, more than eleven years before the treasures of Knossos were brought to light, evidence was revealed of intercourse between the Egypt of the Middle Kingdom and the great sister civilization of Crete.

ANOTHER PERIOD OF DARKNESS

The close of the twelfth dynasty, which seems to have been a period of great and solid prosperity, is followed by the second of the great dark gaps in Egyptian history. Of the dynasties from the thirteenth to the sixteenth and the great catastrophe known as the Hyksos domination, which falls within this period, little is known save from the fanciful and conflicting stories which have been preserved for us in Josephus and other more or less untrustworthy historical writers.

Nor can it be said that modern exploration has done much to lighten the darkness. We know that upon a decadent Egypt, suffering perhaps from the reaction which seems so often to follow upon the rule of a race of strong and masterful monarchs, there descended a horde of invaders, probably of Semitic origin; that Egypt was conquered and lay under the dominion of these invaders for several generations, and that the yoke of the oppressor was not thrown off till the rise of the seventeenth dynasty, when the Theban princes asserted their power and, after a long war of independence, drove out the alien rulers. In spite of exploration and speculation, the Hyksos remain almost as much of a mystery as ever.

AN AGE OF SPLENDOR AND POWER

We come now, however, to that period of Egyptian history which has left us the most abundant and convincing evidences of its greatness and splendor. Quite probably the actual prosperity and power of the land under the empire was no greater than under the Middle Kingdom, and indeed the period of the Senuserts and Amenemhats comes more and more to be regarded as the true Golden Age of Egyptian history; but in the eighteenth dynasty Egypt begins to take definite rank as a world empire, and under the brilliant leadership of kings like Tahutmes III makes her one real appearance on the stage of history as a great military power, while the kings of the nine-teenth dynasty, less successful in their warlike ventures, exhibit a splendor and lavishness in their domestic enterprises which are elsewhere unparalleled in the national history.

The mass of material coming down to us from this time is far greater than that which we possess from any earlier, and far more interest-ing than that from any later period, and it is in connection with eighteenth and nineteenth dynasty history and personalities that the romance of modern exploration has perhaps been most conspicuous.

The power and magnificence of the Egyptian monarchy in this period has for long, of course, been no novelty. Evidence of both was manifest and unmistakable in the great temple buildings at Karnak, Luxor, Abydos, the Ramesseum, and elsewhere. What modern dis-covery has done is to fill in the outlines, to give color and movement to the picture, to reveal to us documentary evidence of the historical processes whose lines could be already traced, and to bring us, strangely enough, into contact with the actual remains of the men and women who guided the destinies of Egypt in these far-off days.

Nothing has more profoundly moved the imagination of the intelligent public than the fact that it has become possible to look upon the very faces and forms of men whose actions were familiar to us from our childhood in the Bible story—the Pharaoh who oppressed the Israelites and ordered their children to be cast into the river, and his successor, whose hard heart was humbled by the plagues of Egypt.

THE MUMMIES OF THE GREAT KINGS OF BIBLICAL TIMES DISCOVERED

From about 1871 it became evident, by the relics of certain kings which were coming by illicit channels upon the antiquity market, that tomb-robbers had obtained access to some hitherto unsuspected tombs. The authorities in Egypt took up the matter; methods of some-what primitive justice were employed to extract the facts, and in 1881 M. (now Sir Gaston) Maspero was led to the mouth of a disused tomb at the foot of the cliffs of Deir-el-Bahari, where, in the bowels of the earth, was discov-ered a most wonderful collection of the mum-mies of the great kings of this most glittering period of Egyptian history (see page 18).

Tahutmes III, the great soldier of Egypt, was there, proving, like so many other famous captains, to have been a man of somewhat small stature and insignificant appearance. Rameses II, the Great Oppressor of Hebrew story and the most grandiose figure of Egyptian history, and, most stately and kingly of all, Sety I, the father of Rameses, whose wonderfully pre-served features, clear-cut and aristocratic, con-vey a remarkable impression of royal dignity; these, and many other figures of less signifi-cance, royal and princely, proved to have been all huddled together in this obscure pit.

The discovery of this astonishing cache of ancient royalties, and especially the fact that some of the bodies discovered were those of men who must have been in touch with scrip-tural heroes and events, gave a great impulse to popular interest in Egyptology. The mummies were found, by hastily scrawled inscriptions on their bandages, to have been gathered in their hiding-place by the priests of the twenty-first and twenty-second dynasties. At that time the decaying authority of the later Pharaohs had proved insufficient to protect the royal tombs from the raids of the tomb robbers, who have always found a profitable business in Egypt.

In vain the panic-stricken priests shifted the bodies of their dead masters from tomb to tomb, recording each reburial as it was made.

A BISHAREEN BOY AND GIRL AT ASSOUAN
The Bishareens are the aborigines of Nubia and an encampment of them may be seen on the outskirts of Assouan, near an old Arab cemetery. This photograph was taken at the threshold of one of the burial grounds.

THE GATEWAY OF PTOLEMY EUERGETES AT KARNAK

This monument, erected by a member of the last royal line in Egypt about 230 B.C., is the best preserved structure at Karnak. It stands at the entrance to the temple of the god Khons, the Son of Amen, and his consort Mut, who were the three gods chiefly worshiped at Thebes. On the other side of the portal is another magnificent avenue of sphinxes similar to that shown on page 36. Nothing now remains of the temple of Khons, which was built by Rameses II in the twentieth dynasty, except a few stones sufficient to show the ground plan.

Each successive hiding-place was violated, until at last, about 940 B.C., they found in the pit of Deir-el-Bahari a resting-place sufficiently obscure to baffle their relentless enemies. There this grim company of ancient dignities slept undisturbed for nearly 3,000 years, till modern science, as remorseless as ancient knavery, dragged them from their rest to become a gazing-stock in modern museums.

A KING WHO RESTED UNDISTURBED

Since Maspero's great find, there has been no discovery of royal mummies on anything like so extensive a scale; but now and again research in the Valley of the Kings at Thebes has added another royalty or two to the stock. The most important of the later discoveries have been that of the mummy of Amenhotep II, the only Egyptian king whose body has so far been found resting within its own tomb; that of Merenptah, supposed to have been the Pharaoh of the Exodus, the actual opponent of Moses, and that of the bones of Akhenaten, the heretic king, which were found in the grave of his mother, Queen Tyi, by the American explorer, Mr. Theodore M. Davis, whose good fortune in this form of exploration has been phenomenal.

The tomb of Amenhotep II was discovered in 1898 by M. Grèbaut. The great king was found lying in state in his rock-hewn sepulcher with its gold-starred blue-painted roof, his bow, of which he boasted that none save himself could bend it, lying beside him. The Egyptian authorities have allowed him to rest in the grave where his mourning subjects laid him; but his tomb has been made the scene of an exhibition whose taste is perhaps rather more than doubtful.

"The royal body," says Mr. H. R. Hall, "now lies there for all to see. The tomb is lighted by electricity, as are all the principal tombs of the kings. At the head of the sarcophagus is a single lamp, and when the party of visitors is collected in silence around the place of death, all the lights are turned out, and then the single light is switched on, showing the royal head illuminated against the surrounding blackness. The effect is indescribably weird and impressive." Some might feel tempted to say indescribably vulgar; and one wonders what Amenhotep's own opinion of it all might have been.

THE PHAROAH OF THE EXODUS

Amenhotep's tomb contained also another mummy, which occupied a coffin bearing the name of Set-nekht. When the coffin was opened the mummy was found, by means of a scribe's inscription on one of the bandages, to be really that of the Pharaoh who is above all others most interesting to students of biblical history—Merenptah, the Pharaoh of the Exodus. Hitherto the absence of his body from its sarcophagus in the royal tomb in the Valley of the Kings had been accounted for by careless readers of the Bible as quite natural, seeing that the Pharaoh of the Exodus was drowned in the Red Sea. The Exodus narrative, of course, makes no such statement, and Merenptah's absence from his own tomb is now accounted for. He had simply been moved to Amenhotep's tomb for greater security against the attempts of tomb-robbers.

On July 8, 1907, Merenptah's mummy was unwrapped by Prof. Elliot Smith in the presence of Sir G. Maspero and others. The face was of the characteristic family type already seen in the mummies of his father, Rameses II, and his grandfather, Sety I—high-bred and

THE FAMOUS AVENUE OF SPHINXES, LEADING TO
THE GREAT TEMPLE OF AMEN-RA: KARNAK

At Karnak there are two of these avenues of sphinxes—or rather rams—one leading to the temple of Khons and the other, by far the best preserved, is shown in the picture. The ram was sacred to Amen-Ra, the great god and protector of Thebes, and consequently figures prominently in the decorations of the city. This avenue was erected probably by Rameses II, who placed between the paws of each sphinx a portrait statue of one of his predecessors. The obelisk at the extreme right of the picture is that of Sety II, a king of the nineteenth dynasty. The great pylon which crosses the avenue is the largest in Egypt, being 142 feet high, 50 feet thick, and having a total frontage of 376 feet. When it was built is not known, but it is probably the result of the enthusiasm of one of the later Ptolemies.

aristocratic in its lines with pronouncedly aquiline nose and strong, determined jaw. Surely in such discoveries the pure romance of exploration reaches its highest point, as we are brought face to face with the actual bodily presence of men whose actions have formed one of the most familiar and striking stories of history to countless thousands of readers.

The explorer, however, is but slightly concerned with the mere romance of his work; it is a byproduct. What he is searching for is the actual historical evidence, which will enable him to fill up gaps in his scheme of history, or the archeological evidence, which will help him to reconstruct the life of ancient times. In these respects modern exploration has given us several discoveries which have been of very high importance in their bearing upon our knowledge of the central period of the Egyptian empire.

A TREASURE THAT WAS NEARLY LOST

By the first of these, the discovery of the Tell-el-Amarna letters, archeology can scarcely be said to have reaped any great credit, though it has been, perhaps, the most far-reaching of all recent discoveries in its influence upon our conception of the life of the great nations of the world in the second millennium B.C., and the most valuable for the reconstruction of the lines of history.

About the end of the year 1887 a woman who was digging out dust for top dressing from among the ruins of the former palace of Amenhotep IV (Akhenaten) at Tell-el-Amarna came upon a heap of little tablets made of baked clay and inscribed with arrow-headed writing. She disposed of her interest in the find to a friend for the sum of ten piastres (half a dollar)! The tablets were hawked about from dealer to dealer, offered to at least two archeologists, and refused by them as being probably forgeries. Many were smashed or ground to dust in the process of being carried in sacks from place to place.

Finally, when an amount of priceless material, whose importance can never now be estimated, had been forever lost, the scientific world tardily awakened to some conception of the value of the tablets, and the bulk of what remained was acquired by the museums of Berlin and Cairo and the British Museum, a few scattered tablets finding their way into private collections. The loss incurred by the apathy of official archeology can scarcely be overestimat-

ed, for the tablets proved to be from the archives of the Egyptian Foreign Office of the fifteenth century B.C., and contained correspondence from the kings of Mesopotamia and the vassal princes and residents representing Egypt in Syria during precisely that period of Egyptian history which is being more and more recognized as the crisis of the fortunes of the empire.

The earlier letters date from the reign of Amenhotep III, the most magnificent king of the great eighteenth dynasty, and are full of interest as revealing the close and constant communication which prevailed among the kingdoms of the ancient East; but the greater part of the correspondence belongs to the reign of Akhenaten, the son and successor of Amenhotep III and the most interesting and pathetic figure of Egyptian history.

Amenhotep III, a luxurious, broad minded, and lavish monarch, who expended in works and habits of splendor the great resources of the empire acquired by his warlike ancestors, had imbibed a great liking for the Semitic customs and ideas brought into the land by the numerous captives and hostages drawn from the Syrian tribes during the long wars and developed by the years of peaceful intercourse which followed. He married an Egyptian lady, not of royal birth, Queen Tyi, a woman who deserves to rank with Queen Hatshepsut as one of the two most remarkable women whom Egypt has produced (see page 23). Even during the lifetime of Amenhotep III Syrian conceptions of religion began to assert their hold, evidently largely because of the influence of Queen Tyi, and indications are not wanting that the cult of a form of solar deity called the Aten was beginning to make headway at the court.

But when, on the death of Amenhotep, his son Amenhotep IV, a mere boy, ascended the throne, the full extent of this influence speedily

LOOKING ACROSS THE GREAT HYPOSTYLE HALL
OF THE TEMPLE OF AMEN-RA: KARNAK

The date is 1200-1500 B.C. There are 134 columns, and the two between which the men are standing in this photograph are 80 feet high and 33 feet in circumference. This great hall, one of the finest achievements of Egyptian architecture, was begun by Rameses I, but he only erected the pylon and one of the pillars, and it was left for his son, Sety I, to accomplish the great majority of the work, and for his grandson, Rameses II, to finish it. This hall is the largest single chamber ever reared by the Egyptians, and, although opinions differ upon its artistic merits, it is certainly among the most imposing buildings in the world. Almost all the sculpture on the columns is due to the completing hand of Rameses II.

GREAT COLUMNS OF THE NAVE AT KARNAK, WITH OBELISK OF TAHUTMES I

The first of the great soldier kings of Egypt was Tahutmes (Thothmes) I, the conqueror of Nubia and Syria. At Karnak, which is a modern name for the northern half of the ruins of Thebes, he built two great pylons or gateways before the temple of Amen-Ra, and in front of one of them set up the great obelisk, 76 feet in height, shown in the picture. Fine as this obelisk is, it is overshadowed by a still larger monolith erected by his great daughter, Hatshepsut, the Queen Elizabeth of ancient Egypt.

NAVE OF THE GREAT TEMPLE OF KARNAK: THEBES

On the capitals of each of the columns 100 men could stand, and the human figures in the foreground give an admirable idea of the size of these huge pillars. This nave is entirely the work of Sety I, as are the columns in the whole of the northern half of the hall. On the outer walls Sety had sculptured, in relief, scenes from his wars against the Shasu, the Libyans, and the Hittites, and in this series, over 200 feet long, are some of the most vivid battle pictures found in Egypt.

ANOTHER VIEW OF THE NAVE OF THE HYPOSTYLE HALL: KARNAK

Compared with this temple of Amen-Ra, even the greatest of modern religious edifices is insignificant. The hypostyle hall was the smallest of the three groups of buildings of which the temple was composed. It measured 170 feet by 329 feet and yet it occupied less than one-seventh of the entire length of the temple. A clearer idea of the size of this hall may be gained when it is stated that the great cathedral of Notre Dame at Paris could be put into it and there would still be plenty of room to spare.

began to make itself felt. Doubtless influenced at first to a large extent by his mother, Queen Tyi, but driven also by the convictions of his own keenly religious and even fanatical nature, Amenhotep IV drifted away from the accepted Egyptian creed and substituted for it as the court religion a purely monotheistic and spiritual system, the worship of the Aten, or vital energy of the solar disc.

He endeavored to thrust his new religion upon the nation to the exclusion of all other cults. The worship of Amen and the other gods of Egypt was proscribed, the temples were shut up, and even the name of Amen was hammered out of all inscriptions. As it occurred in his own name, the king discarded the title which his ancestors had made glorious, and named himself Akhenaten, "Spirit of the Aten." To complete the religious revolution, he abandoned Thebes and built for himself a new capital at Tell-el-Amarna, naming it "Khut-Aten," "Horizon of the Aten."

The importance of the change which the young king contemplated can scarcely be overestimated. It was the first attempt in human history to set up a genuinely spiritual religion and to substitute for the old polytheistic congeries of gods the conception of one universal deity—invisible, intangible, and spiritual. Akhenaten's religious conceptions were embodied in two beautiful hymns to the Aten which have come down to us, and whose authorship has, with great probability, been ascribed to the king himself.

THE HEBREW PROPHETS ANTICIPATED

A study of these hymns reveals the fact that he had reached very much the same beliefs with regard to the nature of God which animated the Hebrew psalmists of seven centuries later.

Professor Breasted, of Chicago, who has presented a brilliant sketch of Akhenaten in his "History of Egypt," thus sums up the man and his daring attempt to revolutionize religion:

"Such a spirit as the world had never seen before—a brave soul, undauntedly facing the momentum of immemorial tradition, and thereby stepping out from the long line of conventional and colorless Pharaohs that he might disseminate ideas far beyond and above the capacity of his age to understand. Among the Hebrews, seven or eight hundred years later, we look for such men; but the modern world has yet adequately to value or even acquaint itself with this man, who in an age so remote and under conditions so adverse became the world's first idealist and the world's first individual."

Akhenaten, however, was a man born out of due time. The world was not ready for him and his advanced ideas. The empire of Egypt required at the moment not a religious idealist, but a practical soldier for its ruler, and the results of the king's devotion to his new ideas were disastrous in the extreme to the empire which he ruled. In the north of Syria the rising power of the Hittites was pressing upon the nations bordering upon the Egyptian empire; within the Syrian province of the empire itself revolutionary and rebel forces were at work, and the Tell-el-Amarna correspondence reveals to us the process by which the empire which the great soldier kings of the eighteenth dynasty had built up crumbled to pieces during a single short reign.

A PATHETIC CRY FOR HELP

Letter after letter came from the vassal princes and governors of Syria, detailing the progress of the enemies of Egypt and vainly imploring the king to send help. The letters of

ROYAL STATUES, PYLON OF TAHUTMES III: KARNAK

The holy of holies and one of the pylons of the temple of Amen-Ra were the work of another great warrior king, Tahutmes III, the half brother and nephew of Hatshepsut, whom he succeeded on the throne. On the walls of his additions to the temple he caused the stories of his victories to be inscribed, together with pictures of all the rare plants which he had brought back from his Syrian campaigns. This monarch has a peculiar interest for the people of America, as the obelisk commemorating his fourth jubilee, which he erected at Heliopolis, now stands in Central Park, New York.

THE MOST BEAUTIFUL COLONADE IN EGYPT, LOOKING SOUTH ACROSS THE COURT OF AMENHOTEP III, LUXOR TEMPLE: THEBES

The temple of Luxor is one of the finest of the monuments of ancient Thebes and is of enormous dimensions, measuring 900 feet from back to front. The columns surrounding the open court shown in the picture are characteristically Egyptian. Each column is meant to suggest a cluster of papyrus buds, the shaft being the stems and the capital the buds, while the plain broad surface below is the band of linen holding the cluster together. The larger columns to the left, forming the nave of an unfinished hall, are of the open flower type, the capital showing the open bell of the lotus blossom. These columns were painted in the natural hues of the flowers they represented and the effect of these vivid colors under the intense blue of an Egyptian sky can easily be imagined.

Rib-addi of Gubla, Abi-milki of Tyre, and Abd-Khiba of Jerusalem are infinitely pathetic in their hopeless loyalty. Again and again they sound in the king's ears the note of warning. If he will only bestir himself, only send them even a handful of Egyptian soldiers, the situation may yet be saved. Such a cry as the following, from a loyal town hard pressed by enemies, moves the heart even yet, across all the centuries:

"And now Dunip, your city, weeps, and her tears are running, and there is no help for us. For twenty years we have been sending to our Lord, the King, the King of Egypt; but there has not come to us a word from our Lord, not one."

The letters drew no answer, or none that availed. Akhenaten was entirely engrossed with spiritual interests. One by one the Egyptian vassals, deserted and despairing, succumbed to the pressure of their enemies; and before the king died, still in early manhood, broken-hearted, one may imagine, by the failure of his life's work, practically the whole of the Egyptian empire in Syria had passed away from the rule of the Pharaohs. Within a generation or two his new capital had been abandoned and was falling into ruins, his name had become a hissing and an execration in Egypt, and the land had gone back to its old gods.

THE CITY OF THE HERETIC KING

One of the most brilliantly successful chapters of modern excavation is connected with the heretic king, his mother, and his capital of Tell-el-Amarna. Flinders Petrie's excavations on the abandoned site revealed a palace whose enclosure measured 1,500 by 500 feet and whose decoration showed the development of a naturalistic form of art unknown in Egypt save during this reign, while the great temple of the Aten proved to be a building 250 feet square and standing in an enclosure nearly half a mile long. The relics of the adornment of the palace were exceedingly striking—a love for brilliant color, for all forms of open air and plant life, and a desire to represent them not formally or conventionally, but in all the truth of nature, being the chief characteristics of the work.

In February, 1905, the American explorer, Mr. T. M. Davis, whose extraordinary good fortune had already led him to the discovery of the tombs of King Tahutmes IV and the great Queen Hatshepsut, discovered the tomb of Yuaa and Thuaa, the father and mother of that Queen Tyi whose influence played so great a part in Akhenaten's religious reformation. It had become almost an accepted belief that Tyi, whose influence was so pronouncedly pro-Mesopotamian, must have been herself of Mesopotamian origin. The tomb of Yuaa and Thuaa, however, revealed the fact that her parents were purely Egyptian; and the wealth of its occupants showed that though probably not of royal rank, Queen Tyi's parents were at least people of considerable importance.

The tomb was intact and the objects it contained were as perfectly preserved as though they had only been shut up a few weeks before. Mr. Weigall describes his sensations on entering the place as being very much like those of a man who enters a town house which has been shut up for the summer. Armchairs stood about, beautifully carved and decorated with gold, the cushions on one of them stuffed with down, and covered with linen so perfectly preserved that they might have been sat upon or tossed about without injury. Two beds of fine design decorated with gold occupied another part of the chamber, while a light chariot in perfect preservation stood in a corner.

FRESH HONEY 3,000 YEARS OLD

Most startling of all was the discovery of a jar of honey, still liquid and still preserving its characteristic scent after 3,300 years! "One looked," says Mr. Weigall, "from one article to another with the feeling that the entire human conception of time was wrong. These were the things of yesterday, of a year or two ago."

But a still more brilliant gift of fortune was yet awaiting Mr. Davis's efforts. In 1907 he discovered in the Valley of the Kings a tomb whose inscriptions stated that King Akhenaten had made it for his mother, Queen Tyi. Toilet articles lying in the tomb also bore the queen's name, and the Canopic jars, or jars for holding the viscera of the deceased, bore, instead of the usual heads of the Canopic deities, four portraits of a female face of peculiar charm—evidently that of the great queen. Accordingly it was assumed that the coffin which contained a mummy wrapped in gold foil and crowned with a golden vulture of exquisite workmanship was that of one of the two supremely great women of Egyptian history.

The inscription on the coffin, however, written in rare stones, gave the titles of Akhenaten, "the beautiful Child of the Sun;" and when the bones were sent for examination by Mr. Weigall to Prof. Elliot Smith as those of Queen Tyi, his answer was, "Are you sure that the bones you sent me are those which were found in the tomb ? Instead of the bones of an old woman, you have sent me those of a young man. Surely there is some mistake."

There was no mistake, however, and the bones were not those of Queen Tyi, but of her extraordinary and unfortunate son, Akhenaten.

When the court returned to Thebes, after his death, his body had been brought back and laid with reverence in his mother's tomb; but when the reaction set in, and his memory was execrated as that of a heretic, priestly hatred pursued the dead king even to his grave. His body was felt to have polluted the chamber where his mother lay. Accordingly, the tomb was opened again; Akhenaten's name was erased, so far as possible, from the inscriptions; Tyi's body was removed from the defiling neighborhood of her son's mummy and buried: elsewhere—where is as yet unknown. This miserable revenge accomplished, the body of Egypt's great uncomprehended reformer was left to loneliness and shame—the usual fate of men who are too great or too far in advance of their time.

THE POSITION OF WOMAN IN ANCIENT EGYPT

The frequent mention of the influence exerted upon the course of Egyptian history by the two great queens, Hatshepsut and Tyi, leads us to consider briefly the subject of the position of women in the kingdom of the Nile Valley during the dynastic period. The habitual view of the modern mind with regard to the status of women in the ancient kingdoms of the East has been that it was fundamentally contrasted with the position accorded to them in Western lands.

"In the West, woman is the companion of man; in the East, his servant and his toy." Like most epigrammatic statements, this statement of the case has more point than fairness. Certainly it is unfair to the chief Eastern nationalities during the period of their greatness, however much it may apply to them in the period of their luxurious decadence.

As Erman has pointed out, the position of woman is very much the same in all nations which have reached a certain degree of culture,

TWO COLOSSI OF RAMESES II IN THE TEMPLE OF LUXOR: LUXOR

Up and down Egypt, at almost every temple, can be found some evidence of the activity of Rameses II, and his portrait statues are innumerable. He seems to have been a character of whom the Egyptologist gets a little tired. Writing about him, Mr. Baikie says: "When Rameses II laid hands upon a building, it was not to complete another's work and give the glory to the man who really deserved it; it was to steal the work of better men than himself and to batter his own eternal cartouche in upon their inscriptions, regardless of the truth. The most valuable records have been ruthlessly falsified by being appropriated to the vain glory of that sublime egoist."

COLOSSUS OF RAMESES II: LUXOR

Rameses II, one of the best known of all the kings of Egypt, was the third sovereign of the nineteenth dynasty and reigned for 67 years. The earlier years of his reign were passed in almost constant warfare against the Nubians, Libyans, Syrians, and Hittites, the latter being his most redoubtable foes. After 20 years' fighting, Rameses entered into an offensive and defensive alliance with them and subsequently married the daughter of the Hittite king. The activity of this monarch as a builder was remarkable and his hand can be traced over the length and breadth of Egypt. His two finest works were the rock temples of Abu Simbel and the completion of the great hypostyle hall at Karnak. His wife, Nefertari, stands in the shadow behind his leg (see next picture, page 49).

NEFERTARI, THE SISTER AND FAVORITE WIFE OF RAMESES II

She is clinging to the colossal leg of her husband's statue. This is a fine example of later Egyptian art (see preceding picture page 48).

unless that position is affected by particular religious views; such as those of Mohammedanism or Christianity. "As a rule, one woman is the legitimate wife and mistress of the house; at the same time the man may, if his fortune allow it, keep other women, and it is generally considered that the slaves of the household belong to him."

"This state of things, which appears to us most immoral, does not seem so in the eyes of a primitive people; on the contrary, the slave feels it a disgrace if she does not 'find favor' in the sight of her lord." On the whole, this view, which readers of the Bible will recognize as that of the Hebrew patriarchs, is that which obtained in ancient Egypt during the historic period.

It coexisted, however, with a much higher sentiment of respect for womanhood, and with a position of much greater influence for women than one would have imagined possible under such conditions.

THE REVERENCE
FOR MOTHERHOOD

There existed in the Egyptian mind a sentiment that could almost be called reverence for womanhood, particularly in respect of its great function of motherhood—a sentiment which is much more akin to our modern Western view than anything else that we meet with among ancient peoples.

The mother was respected for her supreme share in the life and upbringing of her children, and for all the self-sacrifice which is essentially involved in true motherhood, and from the very earliest days the child was carefully indoctrinated with the duty of reverencing and loving the mother who bore and nourished him. "Thou shalt never forget," says the wise Ani in his "Instructions," "what thy

mother hath done for thee. She bare thee and nourished thee in all manner of ways. If thou forgettest her, she might blame thee; she might lift up her hands to God, and he would hear her complaint."

So strong was this sentiment that on the tombs of the Old Kingdom the mother of the deceased is, as a rule, represented together with his wife, while his father rarely appears. Further in the funerary inscriptions of later times it is the usual custom to trace the descent of the dead man on the mother's side rather than on that of the father. We read of "Ned-emu-senb, born of Sat-Hathor; of Anhor, born of Neb-onet; or of Sebek-reda, born of Sent; but who were the respective fathers we are not told or they are only mentioned incidentally." Even when the father is mentioned, it is the natural thing that the mother's name should accompany his. Thus the Middle Kingdom statuette which Sir Arthur Evans found in the palace of Knossos is inscribed as that of "Ate-nub, Sebek-user's son, born of the lady Sat-Hathor."

A CURIOUS SYSTEM OF SUCCESSION

In accordance with this view of the superior importance of the maternal relationship is the fact that in noble Egyptian families the general, though not invariable, custom was that the heir of the house was not the eldest son, but the son of the eldest daughter. Under the Middle Kingdom this rule prevailed to such an extent that the inheritance passed from one family to another through heiresses. He who married an *erpat*, or heiress, gained for his son the inheritance of his father-in-law; and these heirs on the distaff side, *erpate*, or hereditary princes, whose title is constantly displayed on their tombs, evidently formed the highest aristocracy of the land.

THE RAMESSEUM, THEBES: FUNERARY TEMPLE OF RAMESES II

Perhaps the finest work of the reign of Rameses II was expended upon this great temple, which was to serve as the king's final resting place. Before it he erected a huge portrait statue of himself, 90 feet in height and 1,000 tons in weight, a fragment of which lies at the foot of the gateway, at the right of the picture. Beneath the four statues of Osiris, which stand at the entrance of the court before the hypostyle hall, were the store-rooms of the temple in which may be picked up to this day the leaden seals of the wine and oil jars bearing the king's name, which were broken off by the temple servants in the days when the Hebrews were living in Egypt before the Exodus.

The principle was carried to curious and, to our minds, amusing lengths. Successive generations of Western nations have laughed over the well-worn jests whose theme is the affection subsisting between a man and his mother-in-law. To an Egyptian these jests would have had no point at all. To his mind it was the natural thing that the connections of his family by his wife's side should take a deeper interest in his affairs than his blood relations.

When a man succeeded in life it was his maternal grandfather, of all people in the world, who was supposed to take the deepest interest in his success. "When he is placed at the head of the court of justice, then the father of his mother thanks God." The same source was turned to when influence was wanted to secure a position for a young aspirant. A young officer is received into the royal stables "for the sake of the father of his mother." Strangest of

ANOTHER VIEW OF THE RAMESSEUM: THEBES

Writing of the splendor of ancient Egypt, Mr. Baikie says "The decoration of these temples was magnificent. We read of doors made of cedar and bronze, the woodwork overlaid with gold; of steles incrusted with gold and precious stones and inlaid with lapis lazuli and malachite, and of floors overlaid with silver; while the reliefs which still adorn the walls were brilliantly colored, and the inscriptions inlaid with colored pastes. A great Theban temple in its primal magnificence, with all the richness of its coloring still undimmed, and its adornments of polished granite, lapis, and malachite reflecting the brilliant rays of the Egyptian sun, must have been one of the most gorgeous structures ever reared by the hand of man."

all, when the same young soldier goes to the wars, he leaves his property "in the charge of the father of his mother."

Such importance being ascribed to the relation of motherhood, we naturally find that great importance was attached to the state of marriage. The oldest of Egyptian books, the Precepts of Ptahhotep (fifth dynasty), declares that he is wise "who founds: for himself a house and takes a wife." Marriage was regarded as the only satisfactory condition of life, to be entered upon at an early age; and all the evidence, monumental and literary, suggests to us that the ideal of the relationship between man and wife

was singularly high, and that the husband treated his wife, not as his servant, but as his equal.

Of course, there were differences between ideal and practice, in Egypt as elsewhere. Doubtless the Egyptian was no fonder than we are of washing his domestic dirty linen in public, and we are not obliged to accept the theory that the relations of man and wife were ideally perfect in Egypt merely because the documents give us no evidence to the contrary. Still, there is something very engaging and suggestive in the common representation of an Egyptian household—the wife sitting beside her husband with her arm affectionately round his neck,

THE ROCK TEMPLE AT ABU SIMBEL, NUBIA

This is perhaps the most remarkable of all the works of Rameses II. It is hollowed out of a great rock promontory which juts out into the Nile. The facade is about 100 feet wide and 90 feet in height. The two colossal figures on either side of the doorway, each 65 feet high, are, as usual, portraits of Rameses, while high above them the front is completed by a cornice of 21 dog-headed apes. Abu Simbel is situated on the west bank of the river, 174 miles south of the first cataract of the Nile.

while the children stand beside their parents, and the youngest daughter crouches by her mother's chair. A race which habitually chose to have its family relationships so pictured can scarcely have been false all the time to so tender an ideal.

TWO WIVES CREATE AFFECTIONATE CONFUSION

Polygamy was the rare exception, and it is very uncommon to find two wives ruling in the same house at one time. Ameny, one of the

ENTRANCE TO THE TEMPLE: ABU SIMBLE, NUBIA

Over the entrance is seen the figure of the hawk-headed god Horus, but the temple was dedicated to the great sun god of Egypt, Amen-Ra, and was so oriented that the first rays of the morning sun entered the doorway and, illuminating the two great halls of the interior, fell directly upon the images of the gods in the holy of holies. By the side and between the feet of the colossi are portrait statues of various members of the family of Rameses, including his wife, son, and two of his daughters. On the legs of the colossus at the extreme left are inscriptions scratched by foreign soldiers in the Egyptian army during the reign of King Psamtik, about 600 B.C. One of these, in Greek, is of great interest, being among the earliest specimens of Greek writing known to us.

princes of Beni-hasan and a man of much importance in the reign of Amenemhat II of the twelfth dynasty, had two wives at the same time, and, curiously enough, they seem to have been on very good terms with one another—at least the one wife named her daughter after the other, who returned the compliment, and, one fears, caused unbounded confusion in the

household, by naming all her three daughters after her associate wife.

Want of means would naturally restrain the average Egyptian from such a luxury as Prince Ameny could safely indulge in; but that this did not always operate is seen from an instance of polygamy at the other end of the social scale. One of the tomb-robbers of the

INTERIOR OF THE TEMPLE: ABU SIMBEL, NUBIA

Two great halls, out of which open eight small chambers, and the holy of holies form the interior of the temple, which measures 180 feet at its greatest length. The roof of the vestibule hall is supported by eight colored statues of Rameses, with the emblems of the god Osiris; the walls are covered with exceptionally interesting religious and battle scenes in the most vivid colors. One of these exhibits the characteristic vanity of Rameses, as it depicts him, as king, making humble offerings to himself as god! In the holy of holies were the statues Amen-Ra, Raharkht, and Ptah, the gods and protectors of the great religious centers of Thebes, Heliopolis, and Memphis, and, finally, Rameses himself, as god and protector of Nubia. A few paces away to the south is another small temple of lesser interest.

THE THIRD TEMPLE: ABU SIMBEL, NUBIA

This temple, the most northerly of the group at Abu Simbel, is separated from its fellows by a deep ravine. It is on almost as large a scale as the temple of Amen-Ra, and was dedicated to the goddess Hathor. The portrait statues, 33 feet in height, which decorate the facade, represent Rameses II and his sister and favorite wife, Nefertari.

time of the Ramesides possessed two wives, who are gravely named in the legal documents of his trial "The Lady Taruru and the Lady Tasuey, his second wife." Evidently a luxurious as well as a light-fingered gentleman.

Men of the upper classes, as in all Eastern countries, had their harems, where the women of the house lived a more or less secluded life, though there appears to have been but little of that jealous seclusion of them which obtains in

Mohammedan countries. In the tomb of the Divine Father Ay, a priest of the eighteenth dynasty who held the throne for awhile in the decadent period after the death of Akhenaten, there is a representation of the women's apartments which shows how the members of the harem were supposed to occupy their time. We see them eating, dancing, playing music, or dressing one another's hair, while the rooms behind their living apartments have plentiful stores of harps, lutes, mirrors, and wardrobes.

THE SIZE OF PHARAOH'S HAREM

Pharaoh himself appears in all ages to have been the possessor of a large harem. In the wonder tale of the wizard Zazamankh, King Seneferu is recommended by the magician to select twenty of the fairest girls of his harem to row him in his boat on the lake; and no doubt succeeding monarchs were not behindhand in the number of female dependents who were attached to the royal household.

Under the empire the harem was supervised by an elderly matron, and was administered by high officials—"the governor of the royal harem," "the scribe of the royal harem," "the delegate for the harem"—while a number of slaves watched over the ladies and guarded them from undue intercourse with the outside world.

The inmates of the harem were drawn from many lands; and while some of them were Egyptian girls of noble rank, many were foreign slaves. The scale to which such an establishment could attain is illustrated by the case of Amenhotep III. When the King of Mitanni sent him his daughter Gilukhipa in marriage, the young lady was accompanied by a train of 317 maidens, who were no doubt added to the royal harem. This little army of attendants attached to a single queen out of several shows what a crowd of women must have been lodged beneath the palace roof.

The case of Amenhotep is not exceptional, though he was a monarch of very magnificent tastes. The fact that Rameses II has left lists of more than 100 sons and 50 daughters proves that, as Petrie remarks, "his concubines were probably as readily accumulated as those of an Arabian khalifa."

AN EARLY SUFFRAGETTE PLOT

In these enormous assemblages of idle women there lay a great source of danger to the state. The harem has always been a fertile ground for intrigues and plots. Favor shown to one wife or to her children unites the others in a common grievance, and the result is generally some plot against the reigning king or an attempt to secure the succession for some one who is held to have been overlooked. Such plots were not wanting in ancient Egypt.

We have a very full record of the process against certain ladies and princes of the harem of King Rameses III of the twentieth dynasty, which exhibits the harem intrigue in all its familiar features. Officials of the harem are bribed, messages are sent out to officers of the troops from the secluded ladies, inviting the help of the army to overthrow the king and set up a pretender, and the resources of witchcraft are called in to insure the success of the scheme. In this case even the discovery of the plot did not put an end to the machinations of those concerned. The judges in the trial were tampered with, and the result was a highly discreditable exposure of the corruption of the Egyptian bench as well as that of the harem.

Of course, the great majority of these ladies were never regarded as the legitimate wives of the king. The title of "great royal wife"

THE PAVILION OF RAMESES III AT MEDINET HABU, PLAIN OF THEBES, AS SEEN FROM
THE FIRST COURT: DATE ABOUT 1200 B.C.

Before his temple at Medinet Habu, Rameses III built a palace of sun-dried brick, which has now disappeared,
all that is left being the stone entrance tower usually known as the Pavilion. This edifice is unique in Egyptian
architecture; its three stories, flat roof, and surrounding battlements suggest that it was copied from a Syrian
migdol, or watch-tower, and may have been built as a memorial of some campaign against the Philistines and
their allies. The walls of this pavilion are decorated with scenes showing the king in the privacy of his harem.

ONE OF THE MOST SPIRITED EXAMPLES OF ANCIENT ART IN ALL EGYPT

This is one of the pylons of the Great Temple built by Rameses III at Medinet Habu, Plain of Thebes, about 1200 B.C. It shows Rameses in two hunting scenes. In the upper one he is hunting deer, in the lower one wild bulls. Below are the huntsmen who accompanied the king.

TEMPLE OF RAMESES III: MEDINET HABU, EGYPT

This is one of the best preserved temples in Egypt, never having had to provide stone for buildings of later date. Erected as a mortuary temple for the king, it is entirely the work of one reign and represents the last achievement of the great builder kings. On the walls of the temple, which is about 500 feet long and 160 feet wide, are inscribed a record of the war of Rameses against the Libyans, Syrians, and the "People of the Sea," probably the Cretans, together with all the other events of his reign. This forms the most complete historical summary of the reign of any Egyptian king that has come down to us.

was reserved for the chief among them. Even though the king might, for reasons of state, contract an alliance on equal terms with the daughter of a foreign sovereign, his chief wife was still a native Egyptian—in most cases, though not invariably, of royal descent.

Gilukhipa, for example, Amenhotep's Mitannian queen, though doubtless a personage of great importance in the state, occupied an inferior position to the favorite wife, Tyi—a native Egyptian, not even of royal birth, whose influence over her husband and her son we have already seen to be supreme. Rameses II was married to a Hittite princess, "Maatneferura" or "Dawn;" but his chief wife was the princess Nefertari, of the royal Egyptian line, while in addition he was married to several of his own numerous daughters.

INTERMARRIAGE WITH SISTERS

Such alliances, which seem utterly abhorrent to our minds, were by the Egyptian looked upon as both natural and desirable. Marriage with a sister was held to be the sensible arrangement. The gods themselves had set the example, for the brothers Osiris and Set were married to their sisters, Isis and Nephthys. Thus King Aahmes of the eighteenth dynasty married his sister, Aahmes Nefertari; Tahutmes I married his sister, another Aahmes, and Tahutmes IV contracted a similar alliance, while we have seen that our rules of consanguinity were even further disregarded by Rameses II in his marriages with his own daughters. How such continual inbreeding produced for hundreds of years successive lines of kings on the whole so virile and energetic as the average Pharaoh is somewhat of a problem.

In the strange alliances we have a reflection of the important position assigned by the Egyptians to women and the stress which was laid on the female line in the matter of inheritance. The royal title of a king was doubly confirmed by his marriage with his sister of the same royal solar stock as himself, and in the case of a king who was the offspring of a marriage with an inferior wife, his title was only held to be secure when he had married a lady of genuine royal descent on both sides—very often his half-sister by the father's side.

So great was the importance attached to the female line that even an usurper could legitimize his accession to the throne by marriage with a princess of the royal house. Thus after the *débâcle* which succeeded the disastrous reign of Akhenaten, when the successful general Horemheb seized the crown, he acquired a legal title to the throne by marriage with the princess Nezem-mut, sister of Akhenaten's queen. The royal lady was advanced in years, but she was still of the true solar stock, and his union with her was held to make Horemheb's succession quite legitimate.

WHAT DID THE BRIDE THINK OF IT?

The influence of the chief wife was evidently very great. Amenhotep III has left documentary evidence of his great attachment to his wife Tyi in the scarabs, which still record for us her name and descent and eloquently suggest the pride which he took in his clever consort. "She is the wife of a mighty king, whose southern frontier is as far as Karoy, his northern as Naharina." More convincing still is the fact that, on the very scarab which records the king's marriage with the Mitannian princess Gilukhipa, "the royal wife, the mighty Lady Tyi, the divine one," is mentioned on equal terms with the king before the new queen is spoken of. What poor Gilukhipa thought of it is another story.

Even after the death of her husband the chief queen still occupied her unquestioned position at court, was named "royal mother," and had her own special property, under separate management; while some of the queens, notably Aahhotep and Aahmes Nefertari, the foundresses of the eighteenth dynasty, had divine honors paid to them after death for many generations.

On the whole, though there are certain features, such as their loose ideas in the matter of consanguinity, which shock our modern sense of morality, the ideas and the practice of

THE PYLONS OF THE TEMPLE OF ISIS: PHILÆ

About the year 350 B.C. the last of the native kings of Egypt, Nekhtnebf, built a temple to Isis on this beautiful island in the Nile. Most of this temple, however, was destroyed by floods, and the present structure is mainly the work of the Ptolemies. The fine colonnades leading up to the temple date from Roman times, that on the left is complete, being 300 feet long, with 31 columns, each 16 feet high; that on the right is unfinished, having but 16 columns. Through the central gateway can be seen a portion of a second pylon leading into the holy of holies.

the ancient Egyptians in respect of the position of woman are remarkably advanced and rational, comparing very favorably with those of the great nations of classical antiquity. Woman was to the Egyptian not the slave of man or the minister of his pleasures; she was his companion, his fellow-worker on very equal terms, often his adviser, not infrequently his ruler.

Family life was accorded the position of importance which it deserves, and, as always where such a fact obtains, woman held her unassailable position of respect and usefulness in the eyes of all decent men. Especially the relation of

parents and children presents one of the most pleasant and wholesome features of Egyptian life. There were dark shadows, of course, on the picture, and immorality was not unknown in Egypt any more than in other lands; but the Land of the Nile has little to fear from a comparison with any other nation of antiquity in respect of its treatment of womankind.

Our survey of the results of modern exploration in Egypt must close with a brief mention of the light, such as it is, which has been cast upon the question of the Exodus of the Israelites by the discovery of the famous Stele of

IN THE COURT OF THE BLRTH-HOUSE: PHILÆ

Opposite this row of beautiful columns and between the two pylons stood the birth-house, a small accessory chapel, deriving its name from the fact that one of its rooms contained reliefs of the birth of Horus, the son of Isis, and her brother and consort, Osiris. The worship of Isis centered in the island of Philæ and was the most successful of the pagan religions in maintaining itself against Christianity. So powerful were the priests of Isis that, despite an edict of Theodosius in 378 forbidding pagan services in all the Egyptian temples, the cult of Isis flourished at Philæ until about 560, in reign of the Emperor Justinian.

Merenptah. It is well known that Merenptah, son and successor (1234-1214 B.C.) of the great Rameses II, is the king in whose reign the majority of Egyptologists have concurred in placing the Exodus, though the opinion is held by some that an earlier date, in the preceding dynasty, is preferable. Up till the year 1896 no unequivocal reference to the people of Israel had ever been found on the monuments, the earlier identification of the Hebrews with the

PART OF THE GREAT COLONNADE: PHILÆ

Note the elaboration of the capitals of these pillars, so different from the severe simplicity of those at Karnak and Luxor. On the wall behind appear reliefs which at first sight seem characteristically Egyptian, yet they contain frequent references to Roman emperors, to Augustus and to Tiberius, in whose reign Christ was crucified. In Egyptian, Philæ was known as Pilak—the angle island.

Aperiu mentioned in the eighteenth dynasty inscriptions having been finally abandoned by general consent as untenable.

WHEN DID ISRAEL COME OUT OF EGYPT?

In 1896, however, the long-desired inscription came to light. In that year Professor Petrie excavated the remains of the funerary temple of Merenptah on the western plain of Thebes. Among other finds of greater or less importance, he discovered a large black granite stele (memorial pillar) of Amenhotep III; engraved with a description of the erection of his own funerary temple, now represented only by the well-known Colossi (see page 27). On the rough back of this stele Merenptah had

THE SUBMERGED RUINS OF THE TEMPLES OF PHILÆ, NEAR ASSOUAN

Art and sentiment have been sacrificed to the commercial welfare of modern Egypt. With the completion of the great dam at Assouan, the waters rose over the island of Philæ. The tops of most of the buildings remained above the water level all the year round until the dam was raised another 26 feet, when—excepting from July to October—the temples were entirely submerged. Though this constitutes a great artistic loss, the gain to Egypt, through the conservation of these life-giving waters in a rainless land, is estimated at $15,000,000 annually.

engraved a long inscription, which proved to be of great historical importance.

It related to the victory which the king gained in the 5th year of his reign over the army of Libyan invaders which had been devastating western Egypt. The details of the story in the main follow lines already familiar from other sources; but evidence is added that the victorious king followed up his victory by a campaign in Syria, in which a number of towns in Palestine were captured and sacked. The part of the inscription in question runs as follows:

"Seized is the Kanaan with every evil;
Led away is Askelon,
Taken is Gezer,
Yenoam is brought to nought,
The people of Israel is laid waste,
Their crops are not."

Unfortunately this inscription, so long sought for, only seems to add to the confusion. The mention of Israel in connection with Palestinian towns makes it evident that in the reign of Merenptah there were Israelites in Palestine, and the fact that their name occurs next to that of Yenoam suggests that they were in north Palestine; but, if the Exodus took place in the reign of Merenptah, no room is afforded for the wanderings of the Israelites in the desert, occupying, according to the biblical records, many years. On the other hand, no earlier date can be suggested for the Exodus which does not encounter insuperable objections on other grounds.

We are faced with the fact that the reign of Merenptah seems the only possible point at which the Exodus can be fitted into the historical scheme, while yet at that time there were already Israelites living in Palestine in sufficient numbers to render their overthrow a matter worthy of record in an important historical inscription. The only suggestion which seems in the least to meet the case is that offered by Petrie and Spiegelberg, namely, that when the

family of Jacob came down into Egypt in the time of Joseph the migration was not so complete as we have supposed. Some members and dependents of the family must have remained behind in Palestine, and it was their descendants who were overthrown by Merenptah in his Syrian campaign. This supposition is not without its own obvious difficulties, but it seems to remain at present the only possible solution of the new enigma which has been raised by Professor Petrie's discovery.

Further exploration may yield us more light upon the subject. Meanwhile we have to be content with the bare fact that an unmistakable mention of the Israelites has at last been found on an Egyptian monument of the period in which the Exodus is believed to have occurred, though the mention is such as to puzzle rather than to enlighten us.

Vol. XV, No. 2   WASHINGTON   February, 1904

RECONSTRUCTING EGYPT'S HISTORY
The Work of the Egypt Exploration Fund

By Wallace N. Stearns

A THOUSAND miles of river in the midst of a valley of varying width—at the most 13,000 square miles of arable land. That was the physical basis of ancient Egypt. Nowhere is there to be found a finer instance of a country snatched from the sea by the gradual silting up of a channel: a flowing stream, a belt of green, a strip of upland, foothills and gullied slopes prefaced and interspersed by arid waste, the boundless desert.

Through the genius of the engineer Egypt is being born again. In her awakening the land of the Pharaohs is again to play a role among the nations. The filling up of the Assouan dam began November 26, 1906. Statistics attest the usefulness of the construction. In 1877, in which year low Nile occurred, over 1,030,000 acres of tillable ground were left without water supply. In 1907, also a year of low Nile, only 115,756 acres were deprived of water—10 per cent of that so left 30 years before. The raising of the dam 16½ feet and a corresponding rise in the water level of 23 1/10 feet doubles the capacity of the dam and adds 1,000,000 acres to the tillable land of the delta; that is, water will be at hand in the summer months, when it is most needed.

The reclamation of the land, an economic necessity, has created an emergency for the archeologist. Sites of ancient culture are being submerged (see page 65), and by infiltration the soil beneath is becoming saturated, to the detriment and ruin of priceless treasures yet undiscovered. The rapacity of robbers and curio-hunters is fast adding to this waste, though against the latter precautions are availing much.

REAL KNOWLEDGE
ABOUT EGYPT A NEW THING

Our knowledge of the Egyptians is a recent acquisition. Judging from the stories of the Greeks, the reputation of Egypt's wise men for profundity of learning, and possibly from a

A CAKE OF BREAD, PROBABLY 3,500 TO 4,000 YEARS OLD FROM DEIR-EL-BAHARI

misconception of their environment, we had come to regard the Egyptian as ever engaged in battles or triumphal processions, or delving in the mysteries of existence— at all times austere and taciturn. The pyramid of Khufu, massive and awe-inspiring (see page 10); the great temple of Karnak, the mightiest colonnaded hall ever erected by human hands—these had stood as the witnesses for ancient Egypt (see pages 38 and 39).

Pharaoh, noble, and priest we knew. The voice of the common man had not yet been heard. But now both prince and peasant, rich and poor, are made to live again. From the sands of Egypt, the dust-heaps and rubbish piles of deserted cities, from buried temples and forgotten necropoles, new evidence is steadily coming to light. From the towns of the Fayum up the Nile to the Cataracts ancient sites have been explored. Naucratis, Tanis,

DEIR-EL-BAHARI

On the left is the great temple of Mentuhotep II of the eleventh dynasty, and on the right the even grander temple of Queen Hatshepsut, built 500 years later (see pages 72 and 73).

Dendereh, Deshashe, Ehnasya, El-Mahasna, Tebtunis, El-Amarna, Deir-el-Bahari, and Abydos, Philæ, Elephantine, Memphis and Thebes are among the old cities thus discovered or brought out in sharper relief.

At present interest centers at Deir-el-Bahari. Located west of the Nile, at Thebes, this site has become a Mecca for tourists. Here side by side stand two temples of the eleventh and eighteenth dynasties respectively. The earlier, that of Mentuhotep II (see page 71) antedates the splendid temple of Queen Hatshepsut by 500 years (see page 72). Of the earlier structure, though now in ruins, enough remains for archeological restoration. Between the two temples there is a striking similarity. Both were included within one enclosure, both had porti-

coes of marvelous beauty and proportion, both were dedicated to Hathor.

THE BEAUTIFUL TEMPLE OF HATSHEPSUT

The larger temple, that of Queen Hatshepsut, is the product of an age great in achievement and noted for its beautiful creations. Withers fittingly says of this temple: "Except for the sculptures on its walls the temple bears no resemblance to other sacred buildings. Lying at the foot of hills that rise sheer upward for 400 feet, and constructed in three terraces, where the hills slope gradually to the plain, the slender colonnades appear to support the whole weight of the cliffs overhead. Its own

EGYPT 'S GREATEST QUEEN HATSHEPSUT

Her life is one long record of kingly deeds. She discarded feminine attire, wore the crown, and assumed an artificial beard at her chin (see text, page 74).

THE TEMPLE OF MENTUHOTEP II,
OF THE ELEVENTH DYNASTY, AT DEIR-EL-BAHARI

"On an artificially squared rectangular platform of natural rock about 15 feet high was reared the pyramid of the king—a dummy, for his tomb has not been found. Around the pyramid was an ambulatory, whose roof was supported by octagonal pillars, while its outside walls were decorated with scenes of religious festivals, processions, husbandry, and so forth. To the north and south were open courts, and the faces of the rock platform were riveted with large blocks of white limestone, some of them measuring 6 feet by 3 feet 6 inches, beautifully squared and laid. A sloping ramp led up to the platform of the temple, and was bordered by colonnades of 22 pillars, each inscribed with the king's names and titles" (see page 28).

columns are whitish, like mellowed ivory. The whole material of the temple is limestone, yellowed with age where the sun falls on it, still dazzling white in places of shade, and in either instance providing a surface on which the rich pigments of Egyptian art, faded or vivid, are displayed in astonishing beauty."

Hatshepsut's temple is really a tomb-chapel in memory of the royal personages buried in the adjoining sepulchers: Thothmes (Tahutmes) I; his daughter, the famous Hatshepsut; her brother and consort, Thothmes II, and her successor, Thothmes III. Thothmes I and Thothmes II really built by themselves, but

HATSHEPSUT'S TERRACED TEMPLE AT DEIR-EL-BAHARI

"Withers fittingly says of this temple: 'Except for the sculptures on its walls, the temple bears no resemblance to other sacred buildings. Lying at the foot of hills that rise sheer upward for 400 feet and constructed in three terraces, where the hills slope gradually to the plain, the slender colonnades appear to support the whole weight of the cliffs overhead. Its own columns are whitish, like mellowed ivory. The whole material of the temple is limestone, yellowed with age where the sun falls on it, still dazzling white in places of shade, and in either instance providing a surface on which the rich pigments of Egyptian art, faded or vivid, are displayed in astonishing beauty'" (see page 69).

Hatshepsut appropriated the entire edifice, allowing to the men of her family only the space strictly necessary. She called her temple "most splendid of all," and made it her biographer. Everywhere on its walls she engraved and painted pictures illustrating in detail her principal acts. Each successive terrace maintains its own character.

With the rise to the upper platform we come to oratories arid to records intimately pertaining to Hatshepsut, and naively revealing the forceful personality of this most dominant monarch of her dynasty.

THE SHRINE OF THE COW GODDESS

Here on this upper terrace, sheltered by another of the matchless porticoes, is a shrine of Hathor. The covered vestibule is guarded on either side by Hathor-crowned columns, keep-

BAS-RELIEFS: HATSHEPSUT'S TEMPLE, DEIR-EL-BAHARI

"Hatshepsut's temple is really a tomb-chapel in memory of the royal personages buried in the adjoining sepulchers, . . . but Hatshepsut appropriated the entire edifice, allowing to the men of her family only the space strictly necessary. She called her temple "most splendid of all" and made it her biographer. Everywhere on its walls she engraved and painted pictures illustrating in detail her principal acts, (see pages 71 and 72).

ing watch and ward over the secret of the speos. In the wall-painting within, Hathor herself is represented under the form of a cow suckling a boy, protecting a man standing before her, each bearing the Queen's name.

Fragments of a most interesting sculpture were found on the lower platform of Queen Hatshepsut's temple. The complete relief showed the method adopted by the ancient Egyptians in the transport of the large obelisks. Three rows of boats—owing to the disregard for perspective, apparently formed in platoons, three groups abreast rather than tandem—tow a huge barge on which the

HATHOR SHRINE, FOUND AT DEIR-EL-BAHARI

"A perfect likeness of the living animal, reddish-brown in color, with spots shaped like a four leaved clover. Traces yet remain of the gold that once covered head, neck, and horns. Between the curving horns is the lunar disk, surmounted by two plumes" (see pages 81 and 87).

obelisks are loaded. Despite efforts to restore the broken wall, large gaps yet appear, due to the fashion of the natives to quarry among the ruins of ancient buildings, to the defacement of Hatshepsut's work in the interest of later rulers, to the depredation of the Coptic monks, and to the ravages of time.

The delicately carved and colored relief is rich in details—the pilot-boats riding free with their pilots taking the soundings, the taut cable, the swinging oars, the tender under the lee of the raft, and the rear line of craft carrying ministering priests and the royal emblems.

So under the conduct of more than a thousand men came in state to the abode of her father, Amen, at Karnak, the obelisk now standing and its fallen, broken mate, magnificent monoliths, of which the Queen says: "Their height pierces to heaven, illuminating the Two Lands like the sun disk. Never was done the like since the beginning."

THE QUEEN ELIZABETH OF EGYPT

In very truth Hatshepsut had the heart of a king. Her life is one long record of kingly

HATHOR, THE COW GODDESS

"Beneath her head stands the dead king, whom she protects. The living king, whom she nourishes, kneels beneath her form. She is the nourishing mother of the young ruler as she is of the divine Horus" (see page 87).

deeds. Her inscription declares: "Hatshepsut, the divine consort, adjusted the affairs of the two lands by reason of her designs; Egypt was made to labor with bowed head for her." She discarded feminine attire, wore the crown, assumed an artificial beard at her chin, and it is rumored an ambassador at her court had an open road to her royal favor if the matter in hand were addressed to *his* majesty.

Hatshepsut is one of the great personages of history. Her sarcophagus, discovered in 1904 by Mr. Davis, now rests in the Cairo Museum. Hatshepsut belonged to the eighteenth dynasty, in which time Egypt was at the zenith. She possessed rare administrative power, tact, and diplomatic skill. She carried on the mines in the Sinaitic peninsula. She established potteries and glass factories that produced glazed ware and colored glass. Temples were built or restored.

A scientific expedition went to Punt, at the mouth of the Red Sea, or possibly across on the shore of Africa. On their return Theban troops went out to meet them; the royal flotilla escorted them to the landing stage of the temple, where the procession formed to bear the rich cargo, an offering to the god in thanksgiving for the successful outcome of so great a naval enterprise. And this was in the fifteenth century before Christ!

Collections were made of the fauna and flora of the land—giraffes, baboons, panthers, a hippopotamus, and horned cattle. Specimens of plants and trees were taken back. The precious trees were planted, or some of them, at Deir-el-Bahari, on the lower terrace, and a sacred garden was planned for them. Square trenches were cut in the native rock and filled with earth. In the course of his excavations Naville found

REAR OF SETY'S TEMPLE AS SEEN FROM THE OSIREION: ABYDOS, EGYPT

the drainage wells, the mud they contained, and the vegetable refuse heaped within them. Furthermore, artists accompanied the expedition to make drawings of strange animals, fish, and plants of the country.

THE DIFFICULTIES OF EXCAVATION

Succeeding dynasties did little to change the Queen's temple at Deir-el-Bahari, aside from mutilations and some restorations. A landslide later buried a part of the site, and a Coptic convent on the highest terrace added to the debris. In 1890 scarcely a third of the great temple of Hatshepsut was in view. The recovery of Deir-el-Bahari is due to the labors of the Egypt Exploration Fund and the genius of Edouard Naville. Due regard must be had also for the pioneer work of Mariette, 1858, 1862, and 1866, who got as far as the upper platform of Hatshepsut's temple.

In 1893 the Egypt Exploration Fund took up its work at Deir-el-Bahari. Here Mariette had carried out on a large scale his custom of heap-ing his rubbish close to the place from which it came. In this way unconsciously was buried deeper, under weighty rubbish heaps, a hall decorated with gigantic sculpture. Still less did he suspect that here, too, was the royal chapel of Thothmes (Tahutmes) I and the inner court, containing the immense white altar, the finest ever found in Egypt. The work, commenced in 1893 required 14 years to complete. M. Naville has left nothing for future students to do.

WHERE TO FIND REAL DUST

It was a difficult site. The excavator is almost invariably confronted with the difficulty of disposing of his rubbish, especially at such a site as Deir-el-Bahari, where the temple is shut in between hills and necropoles. Here the debris had to be carried to an old clay-pit in order to run no risk of covering either building or tomb. This precaution, heavy task though it proved, doubtless saved the eleventh dynasty temple from burial beyond any hope of resurrection. Any one who took part in the clearing

MERENPTAH, THE PHARAOH OF THE EXODUS, PLAYING DRAUGHTS:
VIGNETTE ABOVE THE SEVENTEENTH CHAPTER, BOOK OF THE DEAD,
FROM THE OSIREION

LINES OF POTTERY: ROYAL TOMBS, ABYDOS

"Modern investigation . . . holds no site to have been really explored till every scrap of pottery which it yields has been collected, numbered, and studied, and the very earth and sand have been painfully riddled through a sieve. The result of all this laborious investigation is that instead of being confronted with a confused mass of facts . . . we are gradually being presented with a coherent picture of the history and the life of the various periods of the ancient Egyptian nationality from its earliest days" (see page 2).

of Deir-el-Bahari will never see any dust worth mentioning elsewhere.

At a distance of 50 yards a visitor would hear a terrible hubbub, seeing nothing but an impenetrable haze of dust, from which would presently emerge a tram, visible at 10 yards, under the direction of a dust imp—another, a third a hundred. Over the high embankment would plunge the loads, and the train, once started, rolled all day ceaselessly on its double track, save for the noon hour of rest.

The temple of Queen Hatshepsut has been reclaimed from the rubbish of ages and now stands clear—ramp, terraces. and courts—and in a measure restored. Scattered stones have been set back in place. The famous historical reliefs are protected from further damage. The large platform of white limestone stands out nearly complete against the background of the yellow cliff in which the tombs were excavated.

In 1903 was discovered the second temple, near that of Hatshepsut. Smaller, inferior to

CLEARING THE OSIREION

"Here was the entrance, by means of a deep shaft, into the underground waters leading to the heavenly Nile of the other world, and here, close to this deep shaft or well, was the National Chapel, or Temple of Kings, dedicated to Osiris, and close to it the celebrated Osireion, with its mysterious inclined passage leading to some unknown sacred goal beneath the National Chapel. The well leading to the underworld was discovered last year by Naville and Peet, under the auspices of the Egypt Exploration Fund" (see page 101). M. Naville, in the white helmet, stands at the lintel, 40 feet below the desert level.

VIGNETTE AND SEVENTEENTH CHAPTER,
BOOK OF THE DEAD, FROM SLOPING PASSAGE, OSIREION

The walls of this building are decorated with noble portraits of the god Osiris and the texts contain constant homage for his cult of the resurrection. No one doubts that the Osireion itself was built in honor of this god of the future life. On its walls are the very decorations which Horus is recorded as having made in the tomb of his father Osiris, and its inscriptions from the Book of the Dead and Am-Tuat deal almost exclusively with this world of the after life.

the first, it is the funerary temple of Mentuhotep Nebhapet Ra, of the eleventh dynasty. On a rectangular base stands a pyramid flanked by a colonnade, the entire structure surrounded by a second colonnade only partly intact (see page 71).

THE MOST BEAUTIFUL
CULT IMAGE YET DISCOVERED

It is from February 7, 1906, however, that the fame of Deir-el-Bahari really dates, at least, in popular esteem. In a shrine 10 by 5

SETY I ADORES THE GODS AND HAS HIS NAME WRITTEN BY THOTH ON THE TREE OF LIFE: TEMPLE OF SETY, ABYDOS

Every great Egyptian desired to be buried at Abydos, which, as containing the tomb of the god Osiris, was particularly sacred soil. Here Sety I erected a great temple as his last resting place, but did not live to complete it, this duty being performed by his son, Rameses II. The walls of this temple are covered with mythological reliefs, which are celebrated for their delicacy and beauty. They show each stage in the progress of the soul in the afterlife and form a mine of information about Osiris and his associate gods, whom the Egyptians called the "great ones of Abydos."

feet and 8 feet high there was found a life-sized statue of the cow-goddess Hathor, the largest and most beautiful cult image yet discovered intact in its shrine. The shrine was built and adorned by Thothmes III, but if we are to believe the cartouche engraved between the lotuses, the two figures are of his son, Amenhotep II (see page 72).

The shrine is lined inside with slabs of sculptured limestone, but the marvel of the tomb is the statue itself, cut from a stone the full thickness of the animal and high enough to reach the top of her lofty horns—a perfect likeness of the living animal, reddish brown in color, with spots shaped like a four-leaved clover. Traces yet remain of the gold that once

SEKHMET AND OSIRIS, RELIEFS FROM THE TEMPLE OF SETY I: ABYDOS

Sekhmet or Pakht was a goddess with the head of a lioness or cat and is distinguishable only with difficulty from Bast, another cat-headed deity. She represented the fierce heat of the sun, typified by the solar disk above her head, and was regarded as a bringer of misfortune. Osiris is here represented wearing royal garments and the crown of Upper Egypt, and carrying his symbol, the crook. He was one of the greatest of the Egyptian deities and the guardian of mankind in the state after death.

PORTRAIT OF SETY, TEMPLE OF SETY I: ABYDOS

Here we see Sety in the traditional costume of an Egyptian king. On his head is the royal helmet bearing the uræus, the serpent or asp sacred to the goddess Buto, protectress of the Pharaohs. The upper part of the body is bare but for the great golden necklace. The curious short kilt, peculiar to royalty, was worn either over or under a longer transparent skirt. This relief shows admirably the peculiar conventions of Egyptian art, which decreed that portraits must always be in profile, with the eye and the shoulders, however, in full-face view. The feet are always shown with the same side—that bearing the great toe—turned toward the viewer, while if an arm or leg is advanced it must be the one farther from the spectator.

THE MUMMY OF SETY I, IN THE MUSEUM OF CAIRO, EGYPT:
HE LIVED EARLY IN THE FOURTEENTH CENTURY B.C.

"Most stately and kingly of all, Sety I, the father of Rameses, whose wonderfully preserved features, clear-cut
and aristocratic, convey a remarkable impression of royal dignity"

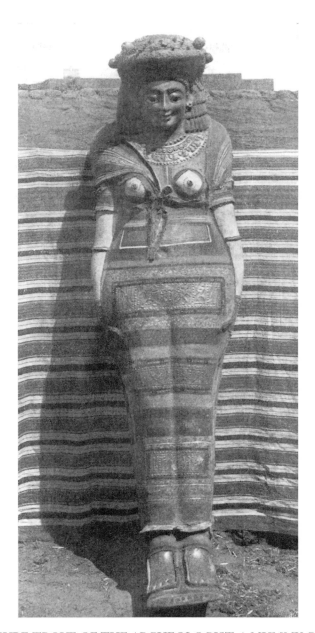

TREASURE TROVE OF THE ARCHEOLOGIST: A MUMMY COFFIN

The coffins or mummy cases of the Egyptians were made to represent the natural form of the body, and were brilliantly colored, often displaying craftsmanship of the highest order. In most cases the coffin exhibited a portrait of the deceased and in later times, especially during the Roman period, these were striking works of art.

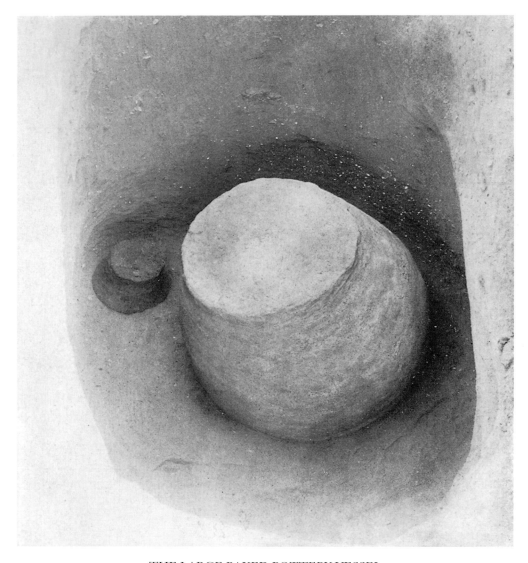

THE LARGE BAKED POTTERY VESSEL
OF THE FOURTH AND FIFTH DYNASTY SHOWN IN POSITION
BEFORE IT IS REMOVED FROM THE BODY WHICH LIES BENEATH
The small pot of rough pottery was found with every burial, but no other objects except a few beads.

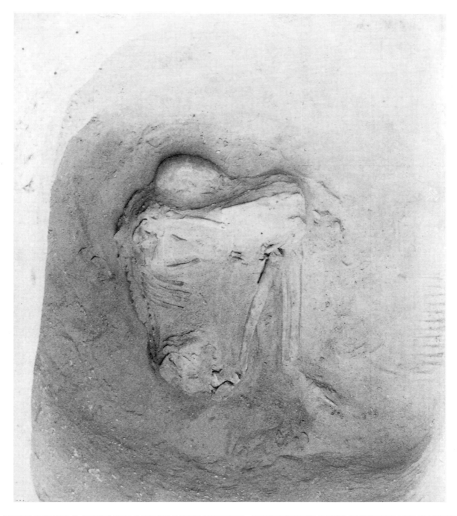

THE BURIAL POT HAS BEEN REMOVED, SHOWING THE HUDDLED BODY

covered head, neck, and horns. Between the curving horns is the lunar disk surmounted by two plumes. A heavy metal necklace hung about the neck (see page 75).

This is the mountain goddess, who from her cave came to the marshes, where she suckled the god Horus. Beneath her head stands the dead king, whom she protects. The living king, whom she nourishes, kneels beneath her form. She is the nourishing mother of the young ruler, as she is of the divine Horus.

About 30 miles north of Deir-el-Bahari is Abydos, remarkable for its location. The high cliffs form a deep recess some four miles across

LARGE VASE CONTAINING 73 MUMMIFIED CATS FOUND AT ABYDOS

and two miles deep. Here are the temples and necropoles of Abydos. Heretofore Menes has stood a shadowy figure at the dawn of history, who merged the two kingdoms into one nation. Behind Menes other names have come to light. We see men, as trees walking, yet we now know that Menes stands at the close of centuries and even millenniums of development.

EARLY BURIAL CUSTOMS

The earliest royal graves are simple, with no tumulus, and having two simple upright slabs, or stelæ. Osiris, who as king taught his subjects the arts of civilization, was set upon by the god Set and his companions and brutally murdered. The mutilated body of Osiris (according to a later account, his head only) was buried at Abydos, the Greek form of Abdu (Abidu), "Mound of the Osiris-head Emblem." Hence the early kings of the province of Thinis desired their burial to be at holy Abydos.

At Abydos are still earlier burials—oval tombs with crouched bodies surrounded by pots, some of which are very coarse (see page 86); others are of better material, even with painted ornaments; most of them of red color with a black rim, and perhaps a few slate palettes or flint instruments. These earliest dwellers—with rude implements of stone, simple ornaments of stone, ivory, bone, flint, quartz, agate, and other like materials, living in dwellings of wattle—constitute one of the rarest finds in all the records of archeology.

These stupendous excavations call for equipment on a considerable scale. Work must be rapid. December 1 to April 1 marks the working year. Every moment is precious. Every carload must count. Every shovelful of earth must be carefully sifted wherever there is a possibility of a find. Even a basket brigade is sometimes pressed into use. As soon as some apparently valuable piece is located, workmen are called off, experts are sent in; every man is on guard. Carefully every inch of soil is watched as the last few baskets of earth are removed. Every fragment must be saved and laid away until everything has been recovered.

Think of the disappointment when, for example, a magnificent statue comes out headless. Think of the conjectures as to the whereabouts of the missing piece and the furor when, perhaps weeks afterward, the lost is found. There is an air of hushed expectancy, a suppressed excitement hovering over, that keeps men up under the most tense strain under which the work is of necessity conducted.

WHAT THE EGYPT EXPLORATION FUND IS ACCOMPLISHING

America has joined hands with the Old World in prosecuting this work. An American secretary, Mrs. Marie N. Buckman, has been assigned to the direction of the American office of the Egypt Exploration Fund, located in Tremont Temple, Boston. Wonderful are the results attained. Every student of history and literature, every student of the Bible, is vitally concerned in the confirmations yearly coming to light from the sands of Egypt.

There is need of haste. To extend the arable district of Egypt is an economic necessity. Accordingly the British government has erected at Assouan the great dam, whose 95-foot head has sent the waters of the Nile back over great areas of hitherto dry ground. Already a dozen great temples have been flooded, and ere long will be forever lost to sight. Already beautiful Philæ, at the head of the first cataract, is gone. The soil is becoming infiltrated, and the stores of treasures, especially the papyrus manuscripts, are being ruined, even before the waters cover the ground above.

Among the agencies engaged in the work of recovering Egypt, the Egypt Exploration Fund stands conspicuous. Headed by no less a world figure than the Earl of Cromer, with such names on its rolls as Grenfell, Sayce, Thompson, Naville, Peet, Griffith, Hunt, Hogarth, and, for some time, Petrie, and a host of secretaries, this association has won the respect and confidence of governments and scholars. Their devotion to the work, their singleness of purpose, their sacrifice, their effective results, and the fact that no organization puts a larger per cent of its receipts into its work, all render the fund worthy of the esteem in which it is universally held.

Vol. XV, No. 2   WASHINGTON   February, 1904

THE SACRED IBIS CEMETERY AND JACKAL CATACOMBS AT ABYDOS

By Camden M. Cobern

Honorary Secretary Egypt Exploration Fund in Egypt Season 1912-1913

I AM writing this in the Abydos camp, with six ibises under my cot and 16 more covering the floor. There has been a great "find" here, differing from anything ever before made in the entire history of Egyptian exploration, and today was the climax of it. Some months ago, when one of the excavators of the Egypt Exploration Fund here, which is this year under the general direction of Mr. T. Eric Peet, struck an Ibis cemetery, built some 2,000 years ago over a sixth dynasty human cemetery, every one knew a unique discovery had been made, yet no one fully realized how surprising and entrancingly interesting it was. No other discovery of the year in Egypt can equal it, I think, in archeological value. Ibises have been found before, but no such wonderful cemetery as this.

Mr. Leonard Park Loat was the fortunate man who discovered and opened this strange and in some respects mysterious burial place, and as a special favor he allowed the writer to help him a little in his happy task of uncovering these surprising treasures. Undoubtedly a worthy monograph may shortly be expected from his pen, authoritatively setting forth the history of the exploration and its bearings upon animal and bird worship among the ancient Egyptians; but meanwhile a little information concerning this astonishing discovery and a few suggestions which may sharpen interest in Mr. Loat's fuller report may not be inopportune.

Hypogeums of ibises have previously been found at various places in which some of the bodies were mummified, notably near Hermopolis Magna, an ancient city sacred to Thoth, and here at Shunet deb-hib, within the environs of this sacred city of Abydos, dedicated to Osiris, god of the Dead. But this particular burial place of the sacred ibis compares with all other burial places as the Tombs of the Kings compare with all other human cemeteries, and as the Apis Tombs compare with all other animal burial places.

HOW THE IBISES WERE BURIED

These ibises are as carefully mummified as the royal personages buried at Deir-el-Bahari,

JARS FILLED WITH MUMMIFIED BIRDS IN POSITION TN THE IBIS CEMETERY

and if it had not been for the white ants, those most successful grave robbers of the earth, we should now be able to examine from this cemetery hundreds of these sacred birds in as perfect a state of preservation as when buried.

Their clay sarcophagi, which resemble in some respects canopic jars, but are much larger, are in many instances thoroughly well made and are exquisite in shape and quality of material. They are generally so large as to hold easily fifty or more full-grown birds, yet are symmetrical and smooth as vases—much better than the jars generally used in Palestine and elsewhere for child burials (see page 93).

The burial wrappings, too, are really quite royal in the quality of material and in the style and design of the outside interlaced mummy wrappings, and they are often made to represent the exact form of human mummies, even to the shape of the feet. These grave coverings are more carefully tailored and as handsomely and elaborately designed as the shrouds of Egyptian princesses. Very few, indeed, of the royal family ever possessed burial garments equal to some of them, the cloth being of finest texture and so perfectly manufactured that even its color is in some cases completely preserved (see page 94).

SECOND DYNASTY FORT IN DESERT NEAR THE IBIS CEMETERY

This fort, known as Shunet-ez-Zebib, measures about 450 feet long by 250 feet wide, while its walls are 30 feet high. It was erected by Khase-khemui, the last king of the second dynasty, and is therefore more than 5,000 years old.

These mummy wrappings have received the most elaborate and loving decorations—rosettes and figures of ibises, and royal crowns and other beautiful designs surprisingly artistic in their color scheme, being worked upon these "shrouds" by fingers expert in the finest needle-work. The intricate interlacing of the black and white bands in geometrical designs recalls Plutarch's description, "The ibis was thought to bear some relation to the moon, from its feathers being so mixed and blended together, the black with the white, as to form a representation of the moon's gibbosity" (see page 98).

GUILDS OF PRIESTLY UNDERTAKERS

These garments are so handsome and of such perfection of execution that the tapestries now sold in Egypt to adorn the walls of modern American homes cannot even compare with them. Only a guild of undertakers or tailors long trained to do this work could ever have succeeded in procuring such exquisite results. They could only have been made by a priestly or subpriestly guild, the members of which had after long experience acquired this perfection in their art. We see here that the undertakers connected with the bird-cult of Egypt had as careful training and were considered as important a part of the priesthood helpers as those who had oversight of the royal funerals.

This discovery opens up a new chapter in the history of bird worship in Egypt. It shows a tenderness of regard and loving homage entirely unexpected. Even the feathers, sometimes with the purple sheen still brilliant, and the scattered bones of these creatures were carefully gathered up and put in mummy form, although the body itself had been destroyed. In one the eggs were also carefully preserved. It is in the realm of the old Egyptian faith that we must look for the explanation.

SECTION OF IBIS CEMETERY AND ITS POTTERY VASES
ALL FILLED WITH BIRD MUMMIES

In the divine days after the reorganization of the heavens and the earth, when Ra left the earth to traverse in his golden barque the shining waters of the celestial ocean and to scatter his beams of light over the two lands, then the majesty of the god Ra spake unto Thoth: "Let us go, leaving heaven and my dwelling, for I will make something shining and resplendent in the underworld and in the land of the deep. There shalt thou register those who did wicked deeds as inhabitants, and there shalt thou imprison them. But thou art in my place and thou shalt be called Thoth, the representative of Ra. I also give unto thee power to send forth thy messengers." Thereupon the ibis, the messenger of Thoth, came into being.

THE VIRTUES OF THE IBIS

Such was the mythological creation of the divine bird. A twelfth dynasty artist has preserved for us his portrait of the ibis in the fourth of the Beni Hasan tombs. The plumage is white except head, neck, and extremity of the wings and tail, all which are quite black. The miraculous bird was beneficent in all his ways, destroying locusts, scorpions, serpents, and the noxious creatures which infested the country, and its searching out and destruction of these enemies to the growing crops and to man himself led to the profound respect which this messenger of a god enjoyed.

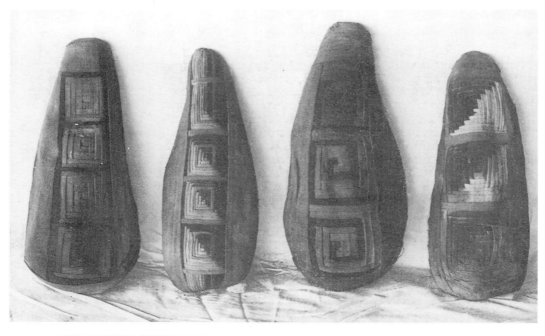

MUMMIFIED IBISES IN BLACK AND WHITE CEREMONIAL WRAPPINGS

"These grave coverings are more carefully tailored and as handsomely and elaborately designed as the shrouds of Egyptian princesses. Very few, indeed, of the royal family ever possessed burial garments equal to some of them, the cloth being of finest texture and so perfectly manufactured that even its color is in some cases completely preserved. These mummy wrappings have received the most elaborate and loving decorations—rosettes and figures of ibises, and royal crowns and other beautiful designs surprisingly artistic in their color scheme, being worked upon these 'shrouds' by fingers expert in the finest needlework" (see page 91).

The 85th chapter of the Book of the Dead, called "The chapter of making the transformation into a living soul and of not entering into the Chamber of Torture," concludes: "I have done away with all my iniquity and I shall see my divine Father, the Lord of Eventide, whose body dwelleth with the god of light by the western region of the ibis." Hence this vast bird cemetery, 2,700 feet square, was established at Abydos, the vestibule on earth from whence to enter the kingdom sacred to Osiris and to the mysteries of the future world, and especially to the cult of the resurrection.

The discovery of the several crowns of Osiris, wonderfully worked, above some of these mummies favors this conclusion. It is also favored by the position which the ibis held in the Egyptian religion and by the fact that the two chief burials of ibises previous to this have both been in cities dedicated to the Osiris cult.

Every hope of immortality held by the ancient Egyptians rested upon Osiris, who had been killed by Set and his 62 fellow-conspirators, but had been brought back to life by the efforts of his wife Isis and his son Horus. The same magic which had brought Osiris to life again, if it could be exactly reproduced, could bring others from death to life. All the funeral ceremonies, all the pictures on the tombs, and all the chapters copied there from the Book of the Dead and the Book of Am-Tuat are for the purpose of imitating correctly these successful magical ceremonies which revivified Osiris.

THE GOD WITH THE IBIS HEAD

It was in the form of an ibis that Thoth, inventor of astrology and mathematics, the god of wisdom and magic, had escaped from Set, the evil god of the underworld. This bird was dedicated to him and was indeed the hieroglyphic of his name as well as the hieroglyphic for "the soul."

To kill an ibis, as Diodorus tells us, was to commit murder and bring upon one capital punishment. The reason for this is seen in this bird's identification with Thoth, through whose magical wisdom Osiris had been brought back to life. One of the common titles of Thoth was "He of the nose," referring to the ibis beak, and he is generally represented on the monuments with an ibis head (see page 99). The ibis was his ordinary pictorial representative and its meaning in religion can only be grasped as we understand Thoth's position among the gods, as the great magician who had invented the formulæ which, given to Isis, gathered together the scattered parts of the mutilated body of Osiris and worked the miracle of his revivification.

So when Horus was stung by a scorpion and died, Nephthys, sister of Isis cried to Thoth, who came down from his sun boat and by his words of power brought him back to life again. What he did for Osiris and Horus he could do for all the myriads of the dead. If properly honored, he would assist these dead men each to become an Osiris, and underneath

his bier, or close to the dead mummy form, we can always in the tomb pictures see this wonder-working ibis-headed deity.

Why were hawks, shrews, jackals, and least one beetle occasionally buried in this ibis cemetery? Because all of these were intimately connected with the myth of Osiris and the cult of the resurrection.

The hawk was always sacred to the sun-god ruler of the celestial world; the shrew was sacred to Horus, who, following the instructions of Thoth, tore out his own eye—the seat of the soul— and gave it to Osiris, his father, in order to renew his life; the jackal was the guide of the dead to the fields of the blessed; while the beetle was preeminently the living representative of a resurrection life.

THE JACKAL CEMETERY

Another surprise awaited us in the Catacomb of Jackals. This hypogeum of jackals was opened by the Egypt Exploration Fund last year and was reopened this year (see page 100). Although deep underground, the stench was so great when it was first reopened that it was disagreeable at a hundred yards distant. The first man who attempted to enter the cave with me was almost asphyxiated, but we crawled out without harm.

To the writer, three days later, was assigned the odoriferous duty of finding among these tons of decayed or half mummified bodies a number of specimens fit for scientific examination, to settle the question as to the exact relation existing between the ancient and modern jackal and to discuss also whether these beasts thus honored with religious burial were all true jackals or whether wolves and dogs were included, for even yet the ordinary modern Arab dog seems half jackal.

I found these catacombs to be almost worthy of comparison in size with certain famous catacombs of the early Christian period used for human cemeteries, while, so far as the number of burials was concerned, these rooms contained more bodies than were ever put in any other series of catacombs known to man. The central passage of this hypogeum I should estimate as being at least 150 feet long and perhaps 7 to 10 feet wide, and this was piled from end to end with corpses from 3 to 6 feet deep, while the many-sided chambers were packed at least equally full.

A GHASTLY SIGHT

All Egypt must have been searched for the hundreds of thousands of sacred animals which were crowded into this huge tomb dug for them in the holy ground of Abydos. Here were big and little, old and young, originally mummified and bandaged and sometimes with fine decorations wrought in needlework upon the mummy wrappings. But either because this was defectively accomplished because the burial place was not so well chosen as in the case of the ibises, or because of their brief opening to the air last year these bodies were all partly decayed and the wrappings rotten.

Crawling on hands and knees for four hours over these piles of bodies, one sees many a ghastly sight—thousands of skulls or half mummified heads; bodies broken and mashed; bones that crumble at a touch; eyes staring wild or hollow sockets filled with black paste; mouths closed just as they had been reverently arranged by the priestly undertaker 2,000 years ago, or sprung wide open as if the creature had sent out a horrible wail in the last moment of its life. The sight of white, sharp teeth glinting everywhere in the light of the candle was indeed weird and gruesome.

That four hours experience can never be forgotten; shoulders bent, back cramped, down almost with face and nose touching these grinning skulls, feet, hands, and knees crunching into a mass of putrifying bones which often fall to powder as you touch them or cause a cloud of mummy dust to envelop you, filling eyes and mouth and nostrils. Modern dust blown by the Khamsin is bad enough, but this is dust that no breath of wind has touched for 20 centuries. The eyes are inflamed as if by fever and the respiration is clogged and spasmodic. Let us be careful, too. If this mummification was with bitumen, it only needs a careless movement of the candle, and in a moment your body and those of the sacred beasts will be offered to the gods in a hecatomb of flame!

CARE FOR THE
SACRAMENTALLY SLAIN

Think of the time and money and energy, the fear and reverence and perhaps love, represented by the mummification and clothing of these hundreds of thousands of bodies, more than are contained in any human cemetery on the planet! That the overseer of the work thought of this as a religious task and had expected the very best care to be taken of these holy bones by his subordinates is proved from the fact that even scattered fragments of bodies were gathered up and mummified when the entire body could not be obtained.

That all these sacred beings were killed religiously and with sacrificial awe must be considered practically certain. To the ancient Egyptian to kill a sacred animal was not only murder, but sacrilege, except as it was put to death sacramentally. To care for a sick animal was as much a duty as to care for sick relatives. A hieroglyphic text from the Old Kingdom makes the dead man declare at the judgment: "I gave bread to the hungry, water to the thirsty, and clothing to the naked. I gave food to the ibis, the hawk, and the jackal."

Every preparation had been made to prepare this worthily as a "House of Eternity." The digging of the sepulcher was well done, and in the walls one could see the niches where the lamps of the hierophants must have stood when the bodies were carried into the tomb and the last rites of burial pronounced. What were those rites of burial? No one living can tell. We here touch the most mysterious fact of the old Egyptian religion, as in the ibis cemetery, the reverence for animals as the incarnation of the life of deity.

WHY THE JACKAL WAS SACRED

Why was the jackal so revered and why was his burial place selected in the holy city of Abydos? The answer is exactly the same as in the case of the ibis.

The jackal was sacred to Anubis, who, in the myth of Osiris, was one of the chief deities concerned in winning immortality for the human race. Anubis was the friend of the righteous dead and guided the soul across the trackless desert to the fields of Aalu. According to Egyptian theology, the judgment came immediately after death and was held in the Hall of Maat, where 42 judges listened to the plea of the deceased that he had been sinless, and where the heart of the dead man was weighed in the scales against the ostrich feather— symbol of Maat—goddess of truth.

This weighing was conducted under the eye of Thoth, scribe of the gods, and of Anubis, the "Opener of the Ways," who stands close to the balance ready to start quickly on his journey with the justified dead, while a little further off crouches the monster Ament, "Devourer," waiting for his prey if the decision is adverse.

The reason why the jackal was chosen as symbol or incarnation of Anubis is perfectly plain. On each side Egypt is inclosed by mountains, beyond which lie limitless deserts. Kings may sometimes travel by the sun boat to the next world, but most of human kind must take their route over the Sahara if they ever reach this happy land of the west. The desert was always thought of as the land of Set—rocky, unproductive, hostile, a land of ghosts—dead souls that have lost their way.

A PICTURE OF THE DESERT

One day I climbed to the top of the *gebel* and started out over the Sahara toward the sunset to find out for myself what this region was that was regarded by the ancient Egyptians as the Shadow of Death. Before night I had become satisfied that the Egyptian symbolism could not be improved; dreary, limitless, with no hint of vegetation or life of any kind, no blade of grass, no bird or insect or beast to be seen, with its imitation wadys and deceptive mirages and endless stretches of bare sand curled into wild shapes; it looked like a demon land, and I did not wonder that the authorized version of the Old Testament translates "jackal," the one inhabitant of this realm of death, by "dragon." This is, peculiarly, the animal of the desert.

Practically every soul must pass through this wilderness before it can reach the blessed oasis, the kingdom of Osiris. The jackal's omniscience as to where any dead body is hidden, his wails in the night as if for lost souls, his certainty of direction out in the limitless trackless, demonic desert, and the fact that though his home is the desert, yet he is never far from an oasis, made this animal the best possible symbol of a guide for the dead.

Blessed even now is the lost traveler on these sands who sees a jackal track! It was only

MUMMY—IBIS RELIGIOSA—FROM NATURE

"The intricate interlacing of the black and white bands in geometrical designs recalls Plutarch's description, 'The ibis was thought to bear some relation to the moon, from its feathers being so mixed and blended together, the black with the white, as to form a representation of the moon's gibbosity'" (see page 92).

IBIS-HEADED THOTH GIVING LIFE TO SETY I: ABYDOS TEMPLE

"To kill an ibis, as Diodorus tells us, was to commit murder and bring upon one capital punishment. The reason for this is seen in this bird's identification with Thoth, through whose magical wisdom Osiris had been brought back to life. One of the common titles of Thoth was 'He of the nose,' referring to the ibis beak, and he is generally represented on the monuments with an ibis head" (see page 95).

last year that a member of this very camp was lost on the *gebel*, and would have spent the night there had he not, by good fortune, found a jackal track, which guided him to the valley. Says the Book of the Dead: "I am the Jackal of Jackals, I am Shu, and I draw air from the presence of the God of Light to the bounds of Heaven and to the bounds of earth and to the bounds of the uttermost limits of the flight of the Nebeh bird. May air be given unto these young divine beings!"

Not folly, but religious devotion, caused the Egyptians to honor this animal and thus pictorially teach a great truth concerning the mystic journey from death to life and the soul's need of a heavenly guide if it make the journey successfully. Yonder far to the west is Khargah, the longed for oasis, and Anubis is the only possible guide thither and the jackal is his embodiment. Let us give him honor!

THE SPHINX CITY OF THE EARTH

Abydos is the Sphinx city of the earth. Only three other places in Egypt can compare with it in the extent and majesty of its ruins, and no other possesses the deep mystery which glooms the strange and inexplicable constructions. Here was situated the oldest sanctuary known in human history, dedicated to Osiris and almost certainly dating back to the first dynasty.

ENTRANCE TO JACKAL CAVE, WHERE HUNDREDS OF THOUSANDS OF JACKALS WERE BURIED

"Why was the jackal so revered and why was his burial place selected in the holy city of Abydos ? The answer is exactly the same as in the case of the ibis. The jackal was sacred to Anubis, who, in the myth of Osiris, was one of the chief deities concerned in winning immortality for the human race. Anubis was the friend of the righteous dead and guided the soul across the trackless desert to the fields of Aalu" (see page 97).

Here is the largest and oldest necropolis of the world, where for 3,000 years the nobles of Egypt came for burial, and even when unable to find final resting place in this sacred ground, here they would lie in state under the shadow of the temple of the beautiful-faced Osiris and bury here some sacred images and make acceptable offerings before being carried elsewhere to their tombs.

Here, according to all tradition, Osiris himself miraculously recovered life after his foul murder and mutilation by Set and his 62 fellow-conspirators. Here he was buried, and for thousands of years pilgrims visited this spot, which, long before the days of Moses, had become the Mecca of the entire ancient world. Here the great kings of the first dynasty built their tombs and filled them with fabulous treasures of art and gold, close to the Mountain of the West, which was the entrance into the kingdom of Osiris.

Here was the entrance, by means of a deep shaft, into the underground waters leading to the heavenly Nile of the other world, and here, close to this deep shaft or well, was the National Chapel, or Temple of Kings, dedicated to Osiris, and close to it the celebrated Osireion, with its mysterious inclined passage leading to some unknown sacred goal beneath the National Chapel. The well leading to the underworld was discovered last year by Naville and Peet, under the auspices of the Egypt Exploration Fund.

WHERE WAS THE HOUSE OF GOLD?

The Osireion, with its strange underground hall, is now in process of excavation (see page 79), and no man living can tell what may be found when the end of that granite-lined tunnel which slopes toward the underworld shall be reached.

As day after day I ask this question, walking around the Osireion and pondering upon its unique construction, the more I am inclined to believe that Naville may be right in supposing that here, within a hundred yards of where I write, there may be found that world-famous "House of Gold," the original sanctuary of the best loved god of Egypt, where, according to the ancient inscription, 104 amulets of gold and precious stones were preserved with other innumerable treasures.

I came here prejudiced against the theory that this was the entrance to an underground tomb or a sanctuary of Osiris. I still agree with those who do not see in the stones so far uncovered any signs of an age preceding the age of Merenptah, and yet I find it more and more impossible to think of this merely as Merenptah's chapel or tomb. What we have already uncovered is undoubtedly a temple built or rebuilt by this Pharaoh—a temple in such state of preservation that it will be protected by the government and will hereafter be shown to tourists as one of the sights of Abydos.

If this subterranean tunnel only leads to a Ka-tomb of this famous Pharaoh of the Exodus, it will be well worth all the effort and expense it will involve to remove the hill and debris in which it is buried. Such tomb would, in such a location, undoubtedly seek to copy the oldest Osireion originals, and would almost certainly lead to most interesting results as regards the religion and the history of that most interesting epoch; but, personally, I am now inclined to hope for the discovery here of the most ancient sanctuary of Osiris.

THE MOST ANCIENT SANCTUARY OF OSIRIS ON THE VERGE OF DISCOVERY

It is certainly not an ordinary royal tomb to which this passage leads. Royal tombs in

THE MYSTERIOUS SLOPING PASSAGE IN THE OSIREION

"It is certainly not an ordinary royal tomb to which this passage leads.. . . If it shall turn out to be the original underground sanctuary of Osiris, or even a subterranean chamber where, in the days of Moses, the mysteries of Osiris were celebrated, and if it shall be found even partially inviolate, then it must mark one of the most important discoveries ever made in its bearings upon the science of comparative religion" (see pages 101 and 103).

POTTERY COFFIN AND DOUBLE BURIAL

This picture shows a striking contrast to the method of burial shown on pages 86 and 87. There we see an example of burial from one of the earliest periods of ancient Egyptian history; here we have one from a very late date. The coffin in both cases is of pottery, but the later form is shaped to fit the body and is large enough to contain two mummies. This practice of double burial began about the end of the Ptolemaic period, and examples of it are not common.

Egypt were never built under temples, and, besides, Merenptah's royal tomb was, as we know, splendidly built at Thebes, where his grave lay close to those of his illustrious ancestors. If it shall turn out to be the original underground sanctuary of Osiris, or even a subterranean chamber where, in the days of Moses, the mysteries of Osiris were celebrated, and if it shall be found even partially inviolate, then it must mark one of the most important discoveries ever made in its bearings upon the science of comparative religion (see page 102).

It is hard to overestimate the influence of the Osiris cult upon ancient religions, and

A MASTABA

The Mastaba is an early form of Egyptian tomb, made of brick or stone, with sides sloping inward and the roof flat. Within were three rooms: in the first was a low stone bench on which incense was burnt and offerings made; in the second was placed the *serdab*, or portrait figure of the deceased; behind and below these, and reached by a well-like opening, was the chamber in which the actual mummy was deposited. The name is derived from the Arabic word for the bench, which is a prominent feature in the first chamber.

Abydos existed solely to exalt that cult. The royal tombs of the first dynasty kings were built on sacred ground and were dedicated to Osiris. The temples of Seti and Rameses would naturally be built over some sacred rite.

No one doubts that the sloping passage of the Osireion, diving into the earth as if in search of the underworld, is in a direct line with the axis of the Seti Temple, which lies above it and about 100 feet to the east, and that it also was built in premeditated connection with the royal tombs, lying also above it and perhaps some half mile to the west. No one doubts that both the royal tombs and this vast complex of pillars and chambers which we now call the National Chapel of Seti and Rameses, were both dedicated to Osiris. The walls of the latter building are decorated with noble portraits of this god and the texts contain constant homage for his cult of the resurrection.

No one doubts that the Osireion itself was built in honor of this god of the future life. On its walls are the very decorations which Horus is recorded as having made in the tomb of his father Osiris, and its inscriptions from the Book of the Dead and Am-Tuat deal almost exclusively with this world of the after-life.

OSIRIS WAS TO ABYDOS WHAT DIANA WAS TO EPHESUS

No one doubts that the relic of Osiris "The Living One," preserved here and carried in all the great religious processions, was the chief glory of Abydos as truly as the image of Diana was the chief glory of Ephesus. No one doubts that the cult of Osiris Unefer, "The Good Being," dominated Egypt for thousands of years in a way scarcely paralleled elsewhere in all history, for upon Osiris, "King of Amenti," "Ruler of the Underworld," "Lord of Might Smiting the Fiend," rested every hope of immortality which could be cherished by the hundred million Egyptians who died during the dynastic period.

No wonder the Egyptians loved him and buried the sacred sites at Abydos under tens of thousands of votive offerings and produced here millennium after millennium the first great Miracle Play of History, which presented in dramatic and realistic form the story of the death and revivification of this "Golden One of Millions of Years."

No one doubts that somewhere in connection with the temple or tombs of Abydos was celebrated, presumably underground, the "Mysteries of Osiris," famous throughout the entire ancient world, by which kings and nobles were so powerfully affected that the grave lost its horror and they could look without fear toward the setting sun of life.

No wonder that one dreams dreams and sees visions, sitting in the dusk close to the Osireion, with the mementos of the mighty dead all about one, and the hope of a future life written big in every text inscribed on every wall built upon these sands.

FURTHER READING

James Henry Breasted, *A History of Egypt*, any edition, is a must. This is a basic work—superb historical writing. William Hayes, *The Sceptre of Egypt*, 2 vols., any edition, is an excellent art history—including sculpture, household crafts, etc. See also Cyril Aldred, *The Egyptians* (1998); Douglas J. Brewer and Emily Teeter, *Egypt and the Egyptians* (1999); Martin W. Daly, *The Cambridge History of Egypt* (1999); Alberto Siliotti, *Guide to the Valley of the Kings* (1996).

INDEX

CONTRIBUTORS

General Editor FRED L. ISRAEL is an award-winning historian. He received the Scribe's Award from the American Bar Association for his work on the Chelsea House series *The Justices of the United States Supreme Court*. A specialist in American history, he was general editor for Chelsea's *1897 Sears Roebuck Catalog*. Dr. Israel has also worked in association with Arthur M. Schlesinger, jr. on many projects, including *The History of the U.S. Presidential Elections* and *The History of U.S. Political Parties*. He is senior consulting editor on the Chelsea House series *Looking into the Past: People, Places, and Customs*, which examines past traditions, customs, and cultures of various nations.

Senior Consulting Editor ARTHUR M. SCHLESINGER, JR. is the pre-eminent American historian of our time. He won the Pulitzer Prize for his book *The Age of Jackson* (1945), and again for *A Thousand Days* (1965). This chronicle of the Kennedy Administration also won a National Book Award. He has written many other books, including a multi-volume series, *The Age of Roosevelt*. Professor Schlesinger is the Albert Schweitzer Professor of the Humanities at the City University of New York, and has been involved in several other Chelsea House projects, including the *American Statesmen* series of biographies on the most prominent figures of early American history.